I0088356

The Garden of the Gnostics

The Garden of the Gnostics
(*Bustān al-ʿĀrifīn*)

يحيى بن شرف النووي

Abū Zakariyyā Muḥyi'd-dīn
Yaḥyā ibn Sharaf an-Nawawī

Translated by
Aisha Bewley

A facsimile copy of the first edition
The Gardens of the Gnostics

Published by: Diwan Press Ltd.
311 Allerton Road
Bradford
BD15 7HA
UK
Website: www.diwanpress.com
E-mail: info@diwanpress.com

Author: Imam an-Nawawi
Translation: Aisha Bewley

A catalogue record of this book is available from the British Library.

ISBN-13: 978-1-908892-62-1 (paperback)

Printed and bound by: Lightning Source

Contents

Errata

p. 35 Sahl at-Tustari also said, "Shrewd men look into the practice of sincerity and discover only that its movement and its stillness, its secrecy and its openness are for Allah alone. Nothing is mixed with it, neither the self, nor emotions, nor this world."

Preface

May Allah bless our master Muhammad and his family and Companions and grant them peace

Praise belongs to Allah, the One, the Conqueror, the Almighty, the Ever-Forgiving, the Determiner of decrees, the Manager of affairs, He who makes the night enfold the day as an enlightenment for those who possess eyes and hearts. He is the One who awakens whomever He chooses among His creation and then makes them enter the ranks of the righteous. He grants success to whomever He chooses among His slaves, then places them among the people of right conduct. As for those He loves, He gives them insight into the realities so that they become abstinent (*zāhid*) in this world. They strive to please Him and prepare themselves for the Abode of Permanence. They avoid whatever angers Him and constantly safeguard themselves against the punishment of the Fire.

I praise Allah abundantly for all His blessings, and I ask Him for increase from His bounty and generosity. I testify that there is no god but Allah. I affirm His oneness and bear witness that all creation must submit to His Lordship. I testify that Muhammad is His slave and Messenger and His beloved, chosen from His creation. The Prophet is the most noble of His creatures from the first to the last. He is the most noble of all the creation, the most perfect, the one with the greatest gnosis of Allah, the most fearing, the one with the greatest knowledge of Allah. He is the one with the most fear of Allah (*taqwā*), the most tirelessly energetic in striving, performing acts of worship and going-without. He has greatest character and highest degree of compassion and kindness to the believers. May the blessings of Allah and His peace be upon him, and upon all the Prophets, his entire family, and all his Companions and their followers until the Day of Judgement, whenever those who remember Him remember Him and those who are heedless forget Him.

This world is the one which dwindles away, not the one which will endure forever. It is the abode through which we pass, not the abode of lasting delight.[1] It is the abode of annihilation, not the abode of going-on. It is the abode that will pass away, not the abode that lasts forever. Traditions and sound intellects provide decisive proofs which are in complete agreement with what we have said. Elite and common, rich and poor all equally possess this knowledge. Both minds and eyes focus on it so that it could not be made any clearer than it already is:

> When the clear day stands in need of a proof,
> nothing the ears hear is valid.

This is the true state of this world. We are warned about it in the Qur'an. We are cautioned to be constantly on our guard against relying on the world, allowing ourselves to be deluded by it or trusting in it. The same warning has come down to us in Prophetic *ḥadīths* and wise sayings. This is why the most cognisant of its people are the slaves of Allah, and the most intelligent of its people are those who do-without (*zuhhād*).[2]

---

1. Editor (Muḥammad Munīr ad-Dimishqī, 1348) Not all of his notes are included. Notes about linguistics or grammar and some poems are omitted.

"Lasting delight" or *hubûr* means "blessing and ease of life." Part of what it signifies is found in the words of Allah, "*You and your wives, delighting in your joy (tahburuna)*" (43:70) which is to say, "Allah has generously bestowed on you an easy life." Not everyone in His path can reach the stage where nothing stands between him and obtaining his goal except to cross over the bridge of this short life, which is the prelude to eternal life. But the one who crosses over the bridge of life while his Lord is pleased with him obtains it. That is why this world is compared to an abode through which one passes, since the believer truly knows that this world is not the abode of an untroubled life. So he is not anxious or downhearted when things are difficult for him, or when his endeavours do not bring him the fruits he desires.

2. *Zāhid*, plural *zuhhād.* This refers to people whose hearts have no inclination for this world. They are not compelled by a desire to harm people, steal any of their property, or to illegally infringe their rights in any way. This is how the greatest Messenger, may Allah bless him and grant him peace, and his noble

The poet described it very well when he said:

Look at the ruins and how they have changed
  now their inhabitants have departed.
Look! They are beyond recognition!

A light rain has fallen on their tracks.
  Their stones have tumbled down and shattered.

Their people have all gone
  and with them all news of them.
Unknown.

When I look and reflect on their houses
  tears overflow and pour down my face.

If I had had more wisdom
  when I pulled myself together after weeping,
what my eye saw when it looked
  would have sufficed.

Trivial beauty is what this world decks out
  to deceive us.[1]
Its treachery never ceases.

Companions behaved. *Zāhid* does not mean a hermit who flees from the world and cuts himself off from it completely until he becomes like a wild beast, or someone who is content to remain secluded in his house or his *zawiyya*, his eye and heart awaiting charity from the dregs of people. The Messenger of Allah said, "The upper hand is better than the lower hand." The giver is someone who goes without because he has been open-handed with *sadaqa* even when he has little property. It is not about taking avariciously. The *dīn* of Islam is one of action, not one of laziness. Allah says, *"Man will have nothing but what he strives for,"* (53:39) and He says, *"Our Lord, give us good in this world, and good in the Next World, and safeguard us from the punishment of the Fire!"* (2:201) What has come down to us about safeguarding oneself against relying on this world is addressed to the heart in order to put the actions of people in order, since by that one purifies his heart and cuts off greed. Greed is the source of injustice and tyranny.

1. This world should not really deceive us because the glittering ornament it shows us in lasts only an instant and then vanishes. Our forefathers were deceived before us, and we have been deceived many times, yet we continue to deceive ourselves by neglecting our intellects with which Allah endowed us to allow us to

Such is it
  that we are not even permitted to taste it
unless its taste turns bitter.

When its ravishing beauty comes forward
  it deceives
and when it suddenly turns back,
  it vanishes -

It is a giver who strips away the gifts it has given,
  out to ruin what it first made flourish.

When it constructs something grand for a rich man
  it builds its parapet against him to destroy him.

Someone else said:

When someone praises this world for his life of ease,
  by my life! he will blame it when there is only little.

When it slips away, man grieves.
When it comes forward to meet him,
  it brings many cares with it.[1]

---

discriminate between sound and unsound matters. We did not pay any real attention to our forefathers nor to ourselves. If we were to understand the reality of this world, it would have no allure because it lasts only a moment. It does not remember the past at all. It is as if it were saying to you in an eloquent tongue, "Cheat yourself by turning to the ephemeral and by turning away from what is lasting. Put your intellect aside and do not turn to what is prescribed. If you do turn to it, then you will see the words of the greatest Messenger, may Allah bless him and grant him peace, 'The believer is not bitten from the same rock twice.' And yet this world has deceived you many times!"

1. That is when it overwhelms the heart. When someone recognises the true value of this world and knows that it was created simply as a field of action for the Next World and a means to it, and knows that what he accumulates of the stuff of this world is actually only a trial and a test for him, then he must use it as the original community (*Salaf*) did. Then there is no doubt that his mind will be at rest in this world, and that he will be fortunate in the Next World since he will receive a great reward and acquire much benefit by his help of the poor. Allah says: *"If you make a generous loan to Allah He will multiply it for you and forgive you."* (64:17) This is what the Prophet Sulayman and the wealthy noble Companions did, may Allah be pleased with all of them."

When a man has knowledge of what I have mentioned and affirms what I have described, then he must travel the Path of the men of intellect and join the school of the people of insight. We ask Allah the Generous, the All-Merciful, All-Compassionate, to bestow that gift on us and to guide us on the path of the rightly-guided!

*****

The purpose of this book is to make clear to you how to travel this Path. It will show you how to take on the excellent qualities I have described. Allah willing, I will mention some of the pearls and realities of gnosis. It will be composed in such a way so as not to bore the reader and so as to render its subject matter easy to remember. Allah willing, I will quote some of the uplifting sayings of the *Salaf*, the meaning of certain inspiring stories and some beautiful poems. In most cases it will be demonstrated whether the *ḥadīths* are sound or excellent, and their chains of transmission will be clearly set down. Whatever is obscure or hidden in them will be made clear. I will provide necessary definitions in order to avoid distortion and to shun alteration or twisting the meaning.

Certain things may be mentioned and then the chain of transmission stated so that it might take firm hold in the reader. The *isnād* of transmission may be condensed and shortened to avoid lengthiness. This book is meant for people who worship and for people who are not in need of the science of *isnāds* and may even rather dislike them. Most of what will be quoted - by the praise and bounty of Allah has an *isnād* which is already famous in well-known books. Should there be a difficult phrase or name in a *ḥadīth* or story, it will be defined and concisely explained. I will not write a lengthy commentary on it because any elucidation of it could well give rise to error concerning its true meaning.

This book contains various sciences of the *Sharī'a*, some of the subtleties of *ḥadīth*, the science of *fiqh* and the manners (*adab*) of the *dīn*. It also contains some of the science of *ḥadīth* and some fine points of hidden *fiqh*. It contains important points concerning belief and some gems of principle. It includes subtle marvels which stimulate remembrance of Allah which should be mentioned in gatherings. It deals with gnosis of the hearts, their sicknesses and their treatment and cure. Should something arise which would require an explanation beyond the scope of this book, what is meant by it will be explained succinctly, or you will be referred to its full explanation found in one of the books of those scholars who possess insight and true understanding. I may refer to a book I myself have written, but by the will of Allah, I do not intend any self-glorification by that nor would I be trying to show off my own books. Rather, I mean to guide to what is good and to point it out and clarify where it may be found.

I have brought these fine points to your attention because I see there are people who find fault with anyone who acts in this way. This is only because of their ignorance, bad opinion, perversity, envy, incapacity, and overall pigheadedness. I want to establish this meaning for the reader and cleanse him of false opinion and reproach.

I ask Allah the Generous for success by my good intention and for help in all manner of obedience. I ask Him to make acts of obedience easy for me and to always guide me to increase in them until the day I die. I ask Him for this for all those who love Him and for those who love me for the sake of Allah, and for all the Muslims, men and women. I ask Him to join us together in the Abode of His generosity in the Highest Station, and to provide us with His pleasure and all aspects of good. I have clung to Allah, seeking His protection. I have sought the help of Allah. I have relied on Allah. There is no power nor strength except by Allah, the High, the Immense in Splendour. Allah is enough for us, and He is the best Guardian. O Allah, I ask You by every means and plead with You by every intercessor, to help me, those I love, and all the Muslims by means of this book. You Who are capable of everything, no matter is too great or too difficult for You!

Chapter One
Sincerity (*ikhlās*) and having a conscious intention in all actions, inward and outward

Allah says, *'They were only ordered to worship Allah, making their* dīn *sincerely His as people of pure natural belief* (ḥunafā'),[1] *and to establish the prayer and pay* zakāt – *that is the* dīn *of uprightness. (dīn al-qayyima)."* (98:5) This means the straight (*mustaqīm*) system of worship. It is also said that it means "based on the truth" (*al-qā'imatu bi'l-ḥaqq*). Allah knows best.

1. *Ḥunafā'*, plural of *ḥanīf.* This is a Muslim who inclines away from fa;se religions and inclines to the truth. He does not turn aside in his path because the *ḥanīf.*is straight. Worship is defined with sincerity, which depends on the heart. A *ḥanīf.*is someone whose outward straightness is a sign reflecting what is inside him. That is the necessary principle because it is not within the power of man to split the heart open to read what is in it. *"Allah does not impose on any self any more than it can stand."* (2:286) It may be possible that a person in a good state may commit wrong actions, but the person who abandons the commands of Allah does not have any of the *dīn* of Islam. The possibility that he will be accepted by Allah is a claim that schemers make to remove their self-doubt. Our *Sharī'a* limits the state of righteousness and the gaining of *wilāya* to someone who has fear of Allah, does what he is commanded to do and refrains from what he is forbidden to do. For this reason, Allah says: *"Establish the prayer and pay the* zakāt.*"*

Claiming to be Muslim without acting in accordance with its rules is mocking the *dīn*, making light of the *Sharī'a*, and belittling the Muslims. It is not conceivable that Allah should accept any rebellion against Him. How can someone like this be one of His *awliyā'* when He has promised the rebels the punishment of the Fire?

> *"As for him who disobeys Allah and His Messenger, he will have the Fire of Hell, remaining in it timelessly, for ever and ever."* (72:23)

Karāma, wilāya and acceptance belong to someone who safeguards himself with fear of Allah by following Allah's commands and avoiding His prohibitions:

> *"But as for him who feared the Station of his Lord and forbade the lower self its appetites, the Garden will be his refuge."* (79:40)

Allah says, *"If anyone leaves his home, emigrating to Allah and His Messenger, and death catches up with him, it is Allah who will reward him."* (4:100)

Allah says, *"Your Lord knows best what is in your selves."* (17:25)

Allah says, *"Their flesh and blood does not reach Allah but your taqwā does reach Him."* (22:37)

Ibn 'Abbās, may Allah be pleased with him, said, "It means that your intentions reach Him."

Ibrahim said, "*Taqwā* is the means by which you desire His Face."

Imām Abū'l-Ḥasan al-Wāḥidī said that az-Zajjāj said, "The meaning of this is that Allah will not accept an offering of flesh and blood when it is done without fearful awareness of Allah. He accepts that through which you show Him your fearful awareness." This indicates that no act of worship is without intention. The intention is that you want to draw near to Allah and carry out His command.

Our Shaykh, Abū'l-Baqa' ash-Shāfi'ī, may Allah be pleased with him, related to us from Abū'l-Yaman al-Kindī, from Muḥammad al-Anṣārī, from Abū Muḥammad 'Alī al-Jawharī, from Abū'l-Ḥusayn al-Muẓaffar, from Abū Bakr al-Wāsiṭī, from Abū Nu'aym 'Abd ibn Hishām al-Ḥalabī, from Ibn al-Mubārak, from Yaḥya ibn Sa'īd, from Muḥammad ibn Ibrāhīm at-Taymī, from 'Alqama ibn Waqqāṣ al-Laythī, that 'Umar ibn al-Khaṭṭāb, may Allah be pleased with him, said that the Messenger of Allah, may Allah bless him and grant him peace, said:

> "Indeed, actions only go by intentions. Everyone gets what they intend. Anyone, therefore, who emigrates for Allah and His Messenger, then his emigration is indeed for Allah and His Messenger. But anyone who emigrates to gain something of this world or to marry a woman, his emigration is for that for which he emigrated."

This *hadīth* is unanimously agreed to be sound. Its position is immense and sublime. It is one of the foundations of belief (*īmān*), its first pillar and its strongest support. It is a unique and precious *ḥadīth*, as is well-known.

Its backbone is Yaḥyā ibn Sa'īd al-Anṣārī. Ash-Shāfi'ī said, "This *ḥadīth* from the Prophet, may Allah bless him and grant him peace, is only sound by virtue of its having come by way of 'Alqama, and only sound by virtue of having come from 'Alqama by way of Yaḥyā ibn Sa'īd. From Yaḥyā, the transmission of it spreads out to more than 200 men, most of whom are Imams."

Imam al-Bukhārī related it in his *Ṣaḥīḥ* in seven places. He related it at the beginning of his book, and in the chapters on belief, marriage, freeing slaves, emigration, giving up deception and oaths. This *ḥadīth* is related in the *Ṣaḥīḥ* in various ways: "Indeed actions only go by intentions," and "Indeed action is only by the intention." At the beginning of the Book of Shihāb, it reads, "Actions are by intentions," and does not include the word "indeed." However, Abū Mūsā al-Isfahānī said that the *isnād* of transmission for this version is not sound. The meaning of the intention is to aim for the goal. It is the heart's resolve.[1] "Indeed"

1. "The heart's resolve": the intention is something that refers to the aim of the heart, not to the tongue and what it articulates. Some of the *fuqahā'* consider articulation of the intention to be part of the perfection of worship, and to be a *sunna* in the prayer. However, the position of the Shāfi'ī school is that the intention naturally accompanies the beginning of the action, unless it is not possible for it to accompany it, as in the case of fasting. The beginning of the prayer is the *takbīr al-iḥrām*, saying "*Allāhu akbar*", so how can someone articulate the intention at the same time he is uttering the *takbīr*? As for saying it before the *takbīr*, the prayer is not yet started. Even if we were to state that it helps the heart, this is not desirable. You often find people who make a great noise in their intention to perform the prayer in congregation, sometimes to such an extent that the people cannot follow the Imam, and he may go into *rukū'* before the people are aware of it because they are distracted by the uproar of this person uttering his initial intention. Beginning like this is not compatible with the stillness which the *Sharī'a* demands of the person in his prayer. Neither the *Sunna* nor the books on the life of the Prophet transmit to us that the Companions or the righteous *Salaf* made this loud noise which exists today in mosques during prayers. It has not come down to us in the *Sharī'a*, and it does not befit the submission and humility required of the slave in the prayer. It is incompatible with the *adab* of standing in the presence of

is used to express limitation. It affirms what is mentioned, and rejects everything else. The meaning of the *ḥadīth* is that the actions of the *Sharī'a* are only valid by intention. As for the one whose goal is the pleasure of Allah by his emigration,[1] and as for the one whose goal is this world, both of them obtain only that portion.

According to this *ḥadīth*, the intention is a precondition for *wuḍū'*, *ghusl*, *tayammum*, prayer, *zakāt*, fasting, retreat, *ḥajj*, etc. Muḥammad ibn Idrīs ash-Shāfi'ī, may Allah be pleased with him, said, "This *ḥadīth* contains seventy areas of the science of law (*fiqh*)." He also said, "This *ḥadīth* contains one-third of knowl-

---

his Lord. I think that the person doing the prayer should be humble and still and avoid anything more than what is absolutely necessary. Is this not more fitting for the prayer? Some people are so filled with doubt that they repeat the prayer many times, thinking that it was invalid because the intention was doubtful. This poor person does not know that what the giver of the *Sharī'a* meant by intention is the person's aim in directing his resolution completely toward what he is doing.

1. "Emigration" is emigration from the land of disbelief to the land of Islam necessary? It is not lawful for the Muslim to live in the abode of disbelief. These days the unbelievers have overrun the greater part of lands belonging to the Muslim and, in fact, they now rule them. The rest of the Muslim lands have been taken over by their influence. Denying that this is true out of a sense of mere self-importance does the Muslims no good. The writer related in his commentary on this *hadith* in *The Forty of an-Nawawī* from al-Māwardī that someone who lives with his family and his tribe in the abode of disbelief and is able to demonstrate that his *dīn* is intact is not permitted to practise emigration (*hijra*) because the place he is already in is the abode of Islam. Following this principle is the best way to establish Islam in the abode of disbelief, since calling people to Islam without any struggle is dangerous. If only we would do what al-Māwardī said, then we would recognise their hearts and the spite they have against Islam. Then we would also come to know the means the unbelievers use to corrupt the Muslims and overcome their intellects. We must not despair of reviving the past glory of Islam in our time. Islam does not allow submission to the enemy and cowardice. It calls for bold actions, courage and meaningful display of strength both in advance and in retreat in every state. We must recognise that the lack of these is the main reason for the loss of our power and the reason for the enemy's victory over us. There must be groups of people calling to Islam who live in Europe and America, who follow the pure, original path, able to preserve their *dīn* so long as freedom of religion is preserved and the life of the inhabitant is not in danger.

edge." Aḥmad ibn Ḥanbal, may Allah be pleased with him, stated, "It contains a third of knowledge." Others have mentioned this *ḥadīth* in the same way.

Abū Bakr al-Bayhaqī said in the beginning of his book, *The Summary of the Sunan*, "What ash-Shāfi'ī meant about the fact that it contains a third of knowledge derives from the fact that the slave acquires everything by means of his heart, his tongue and his intentions. The intention is one of the divisions of his acquisition, but it is the most predominant of the three, because it is worship on its own. The other two are not. Words and actions can be perverted by showing-off. But this does not affect intention in any way."

The scholars recommend that you begin all books with this *ḥadīth*. Al-Bukhārī is among those who began their books with it. It is the first *ḥadīth* in his *Ṣaḥīḥ* Collection, which is the soundest book after the Book of Allah. Abū Sa'īd 'Abdu'r-Raḥmān ibn Mahdī said, "If I had written a book I would have started every chapter with this *ḥadīth*." He also said, "Whoever desires to write a book should begin it with this *ḥadīth*." At the beginning of *Information about the Commentary on the Ṣaḥīḥ of al-Bukhārī*, al-Khaṭṭābī said, "Our previous shaykhs recommended that we put the *ḥadīth*, "Actions are by intentions", at the start of all matters of the *dīn* that we write, since it is generally needed in all aspects of the *dīn*."

We have heard many things like this from the early Muslims regarding this *ḥadīth*. Allah knows best. The chain of transmission (*isnād*) of this *ḥadīth* is considered very esteemed and excellent by the people of *ḥadīth*. This is due to the fact that its chain of transmission includes three Followers, each one relating the *ḥadīth* from the others. These three Followers are: Yaḥyā ibn Sa'īd al-Anṣārī, Muḥammad ibn Ibrāhīm at-Taymī and 'Alqama ibn Waqqāṣ. Although this is marvellous, there are several sound *ḥadīths* that have three Followers relating the *ḥadīth* from one another, and there are even some that include four Followers in the chain. Ibn 'Abdu'r-Raḥmān gathered them all together in a section of his book. I have transmitted it and condensed it at the beginning of my commentary on the *Ṣaḥīḥ* of al-Bukhārī. I added some others to them which I found to be like them. There were more than thirty *ḥadīths* of this kind, but Allah knows best.

Now let us turn to those *ḥadīths* which are said to be the basis of Islam and the roots of the *dīn*. They are Islam's bedrock, and the core of the science of law and knowledge. We will mention them in this section because one of them is the *ḥadīth*, "Indeed actions only go by intentions." They are very important, and should be the first to be dealt it. Scholars have differed a great deal about their number. Shaykh Abū 'Amr 'Uthmān ibn 'Abdu'r-Raḥmān (known as Ibn aṣ-Ṣalāḥ) attempted to compile them and distinguish which they are. I can add nothing whatsoever to his precision and perfection. I have just condensed some of what he mentioned, and added a bit to it which he did not mention.

"The *dīn* is good counsel."[1]

---

1. The Messenger of Allah, may Allah bless him and grant him peace, used to make a contract with whomever came to him to submit to Islam based on faithfulness and good counsel to the Muslims. The command to give good counsel comes openly many times in different *ḥadīths*. One of the people who offered allegiance to the Prophet, may Allah bless him and grant him peace, on that basis was Jarīr ibn 'Abdullāh al-Bajalī. He addressed the people of Kūfa on the day that al-Mughīra ibn Shu'ba died in 50 AH: "I came to the Prophet, may Allah bless him and grant him peace, and asked him, 'Shall I offer allegiance in Islam?' He stipulated the condition of good counsel to every Muslim. I gave allegiance to him on that basis." Al-Bukhārī also related it at the end of the Book of Belief. That is because when you counsel someone, that indicates your love for him. You want him to benefit in what he is doing and make him avoid anything harmful. When the Muslims' love for one another spreads out and sincere good counsel becomes universal, then strength, victory and support envelop them. This is the secret which was given to the Muslims after the death of the Prophet. They overcame the Greeks and the Persians and conquered most of the lands of the world because, by means of the strength of good counsel, they were able to understand the *āyat*: *"The believers are brothers."* (49:10)

Then they become as described in another *ḥadīth*, "The believers are like one body. When one part of it complains, the rest of the parts of the body call on each other with fever and sleeplessness." This is the peak of strength which cannot be either resisted or disputed, just as the hardness of metals is based on the strength of their cohesion and solidity. Iron is only stronger than other metals and able to be used the way it is because of its purity and being free of other metals which are incompatible with it, as well as by the strength with which its molecules are inter-

Part of good counsel lies in attributing the benefit received to the one who gave it. Whoever does that adds to his knowledge and his state. But whoever omits that or plagiarizes from someone should not profit by his knowledge,[1] nor will he receive any blessing in his state. The people of knowledge and favour continue to ascribe benefits to the ones who gave the good counsel. We ask Allah for success in this always!

After weighing what the various Imams have said about which *ḥadīths* are central to Islam and after considering their disagreement about their number, and which *ḥadīths* they actually are, Shaykh Abū 'Amr (Ibn aṣ-Ṣalāḥ) said, "I arrived at twenty-six *ḥadīths*."

1. The *ḥadīth* already mentioned:

> "Indeed, actions only go by intentions. Everyone gets what they intend. Anyone, therefore, who emigrates for Allah and His Messenger, then his emigration is indeed for Allah and His Messenger. But anyone who emigrates to gain something of this world or to marry a woman, his emigration is for that for which he emigrated."

2. 'Ā'isha, may Allah be pleased with her, said that the Messenger of Allah, may Allah bless him and grant him peace, said:

---

connected. The strength of the Muslims is only obtained by their good counsel and love for each other.

1. The one who ascribes someone else's words to himself will not profit by it, because he has failed to keep the trust, which is to attribute knowledge to the one who said it. It is well-known that if someone intentionally commits a breach of trust of this kind, that nullifies any action in which it is used, and it strips it of all good and blessing. It is quite possible that Allah will punish that plagiarist who reaps undeserved benefits since such is the recompense for this kind of action. Acting in this way inevitably leads to impeding knowledge through severing its chain of transmission, failing to give credit to the people upon which it is based, and negating the glory of the *Salaf*.

"If anyone introduces an innovation in this affair of ours which is not part of it, it will be rejected."[1]

Everyone agrees that this *ḥadīth* is sound. Al-Bukhārī and Muslim related it in their *Ṣaḥīḥ* collections. In the version in Muslim, it says, "If anyone originates something which is not in accordance with this affair of ours it will be rejected."

3. An-Nu'mān ibn Bashīr, may Allah be pleased with him, reported that he heard the Messenger of Allah, may Allah bless him and grant him peace, say:

---

1. This means if he says something which is not integral to it, since everything that is not consistent with the spirit of the *dīn* is false and not accepted. It does not mean that everything must rigidly continue in the same state, for that is contrary to the *sunna* of Allah which is a creation continually in flux. It is certain that this is only concerned with acts of worship. As far as the basic needs of life or business matters are concerned, the introduction of new elements are acceptable so long as they do not harm the *dīn*, or bring evil or destruction to the Muslims because of them, even if the consequences do not come into play until much later. For example, when Salmān al-Fārisī explained the trench to the Prophet, he accepted it based on Salmān's opinion, and the Prophet personally began to dig it, even though the use of a trench in warfare did not exist before among the Arabs, and they did not recognise its value. But the aim was noble to preserve the Muslims from the evil of their enemies.

When 'Umar saw intrigues among the Muslim community, he forbade people to travel except by permission given for a specific length of time on a signed document. Today, this is known as a "passport" which means permission to travel.

When the Muslims saw that they had no dating which they could use to record their events, their agreed to adopt the *Hijra* dating, beginning from the time of the Prophet's emigration to Madina from Makka. It was used to preserve the recording of events and the records of provisions under 'Umar, but all of this did not exist at the time of the Prophet. However, it was for the general good of the Muslims, so the noble Companions accepted it with joy and satisfaction.

What the Messenger of Allah, may Allah bless him and grant him peace, meant by his command was to follow the Book of Allah and the *Sunna* of the Messenger, and to look for what would help the Muslims and reject anything that was destructive or false. Anyone who introduces anything destructive or false is someone who opposes the *Sharī'a,* or what is transmitted from the Prophet, or someone who derives some harmful thing from its introduction which can be used against the Muslims.

"The *ḥalāl* is clear and the *ḥarām* is clear. But between the two there are ambiguous matters about which most people have no knowledge. Whoever exercises caution with regard to what is ambiguous shows prudence in respect of his dīn and his honour."[1] Whoever gets involved in the ambiguous things is like a herdsman who grazes his animals near a private preserve. He bound to enter it. Every king has a private preserve and the private preserve of Allah on His earth are the things that He has made forbidden. There is a lump of flesh in the body, the nature of which is that when it is sound, the entire body is sound, and when it is corrupt, the entire body is corrupt. It is the heart."

Everyone agrees that this is a sound *ḥadīth* and it is related in the two *Ṣaḥīḥ* collections.

4. 'Abdullāh ibn Mas'ūd, may Allah be pleased with him, reported that the Messenger of Allah, may Allah bless him and grant him peace, the truthful and confirmed one, told him:

---

1. The Prophet, may Allah bless him and grant him peace, said, "his honour" because when someone does something that is doubtful, he makes an opening for fools to attack him with lies and slander and then they can claim that he has done something *ḥarām*. So he has made his honour a target open to attack, rebuke and slander, and it becomes a reason for them to fall into wrong action. The Prophet, may Allah bless him and grant him peace, also said, "The one who believes in Allah and the Last Day should not get into situations which provoke suspicion." 'Ali said, "Beware! Whatever comes first to the heart affects it. Even if he has an excuse, there are many people who listen who will reject and not hear his excuse." So someone like this is drawn on little by little until he comes to the *ḥarām*, even if he has a strong will and firm intention. And another *ḥadīth* indicates: "Allah curses the thief who steals an egg and his hand is cut off and then he steals a camel so his other hand is cut off." In this, he goes from an egg to a camel, the action issuing from what preceded it, or by having been repeated many times before. Allah says in the Qur'an: *"They killed the Prophets without any right to do so. That was because they disobeyed and went beyond the limits."* (3:112) He means by this that they went from rebellion to killing the Prophets.

"The way that each of you is created is that you are gathered in your mother's womb for forty days as a sperm-drop and then for a similar length of time as a blood-clot and then for a similar length of time as a lump of flesh. Then an angel is sent and he breathes the spirit (*rūḥ*) into you and is encharged with four commandments: to write down your provision, your life-span, your actions, and whether you will be happy or wretched. By Him, apart from Whom there is no god, one of you can do the actions of someone destined for the Garden until there is only an arm's length between him and it, and then what is written will overtake him and he will do the actions of someone destined for the Fire and enter it."[1] And one of you can do the actions of someone destined for the Fire until there is only an arm's length between him and it, and then what is written will overtake him and he will do the actions of someone destined for the Garden and enter it."

Al-Bukhārī and Muslim related it in their *Ṣaḥīḥ* collections.

5. Al-Ḥasan ibn 'Alī, may Allah be pleased with him, said, "I remember that the Messenger of Allah, may Allah bless him and grant him peace, stated:

1. The author said in his *Commentary on the Forty* in reference to this *ḥadīth* that the seal of whoever believes and does sincere right actions can only be good. The evil seal comes to the one whose actions are bad, or someone who mixes bad actions with sound actions based on some kind of hypocrisy and desire for reputation. It is also indicated by this *ḥadīth*, "One of you may perform the actions of the Garden in what he shows to people," i.e. in what he presents to them of a good outward appearance while his secret is foul and corrupt. Allah knows best.

As for the one who performs the actions of the Fire, he may have sincerity for Islam and the Muslims beyond his own worship, and his actions will bring about results of general benefit in accord with what the Prophet, may Allah bless him and grant him peace, intended, but these actions will originate from something other than personal worship. It is a blessing from Allah and he is repaid for what he has performed of good actions and restraining harm. Allah grants him success in those actions in which people see the sign of success, so he enters the Garden by the favour and generosity of Allah.

"Leave what gives you doubt for what gives you no doubt."[1]

It is a sound *ḥadīth.* At-Tirmidhī and an-Nasā'ī related it. At-Tirmidhī said that it is a sound *ḥadīth.*

6. Abū Hurayra, may Allah be pleased with him, reported that the Messenger of Allah, may Allah bless him and grant him peace, said:

"Part of the excellence of a man's Islam is his leaving alone what does not concern him."[2]

It is an excellent *ḥadīth.* At-Tirmidhī and Ibn Mājah related it.

7. Anas ibn Mālik, may Allah be pleased with him, reported that the Prophet, may Allah bless him and grant him peace, said,

---

1. What does not give you doubt is whatever the soul trusts and the heart finds itself at peace with. Wābiṣa reported that the Prophet, may Allah bless him and grant him peace, said, "Consult your heart, even if the person who is asked gives a decision in your favour." Man has more knowledge of what is inside himself, and his spirit naturally flees from injury, since it cannot be deceived by wrong actions. When it is polished clean by fearful awareness of Allah (*taqwā*), then it only inclines to what brings it profit, thereby pleasing Allah and His Messenger.

2. This means to direct a man's action to what is particular to him or is consistent with his particular tasting and receptiveness. If a man tries to investigate everything, whether or not it has any connection with himself, he will be prevented from true action. The balance is shattered and chaos reigns over actions, because permitting censured actions to people allows him to do anything he pleases.

The *Sharī'a* of Islam is universal. No one is exempt from its rules and the only superiority anyone has over anyone else is through *taqwā* and obeying the commands of Allah. If he becomes occupied with things that do not concern him, his actions will become unsound and unbalanced. This is one of the major factors which hold us back today, making us tools manipulated by others. However, it should not enter into your thoughts that what this *ḥadīth* says should prevent us commanding what is correct and forbidding what is objectionable. We seek refuge with Allah from that! That is an absolute command to the Muslims, since the harm which comes from the spread of the objectionable does not pertain to any one individual. Rather it is like a contagious disease. I should imagine that

"Not one of you will believe until he desires for his brother what he desires for himself."[1]

It is agreed to be sound.

8. Abū Hurayra, may Allah be pleased with him, said:

"The Messenger of Allah, may Allah bless him and grant him peace, said, 'O people! Allah is good and He only accepts the good. Allah gives the same command to the believers that He gives the Messengers. Allah

---

the people who oppose commanding the correct and forbidding the objectionable would nevertheless agree that when the existence of an epidemic is suspected in a city, special quarantine places should be built and the city should be put under constant supervision. It is an indisputable fact that sickness in the selves is a stronger force in its attack on the body of a community than any outward sickness. When an outward sickness occurs, since it is physical, man flees from it and takes precautions against it. But as for what man does not see, it proceeds apace while no one pays attention to its destructiveness. Man should not involve himself in matters in which neither he nor the community derive any harm or benefit. As for that which does bring about harm or benefit, one must act. If you see your neighbour setting fire to his house, you do not say, "It doesn't concern me," since your own house is then exposed to destruction by its flames.

1. "Not one of you will believe until he wants for his brother..." because the *dīn* does not call just one person, nor is it just a specific individual right. Muslims are all one in the *dīn*. If someone does not love his companion, that may be because of love of this world, in which case he prefers this world to the *dīn*, or it may be because of his *dīn*, in which case he is envious of his brother, seeking to remove what his brother has, and not pleased with what Allah has allotted him. All the Muslims are like a single body, so lack of love is a sure sign of separation, and separation precedes obliteration and destruction. It is as if he wished to obliterate the *dīn* itself by his lack of love for his brother. This is absolutely incompatible with belief.

In the *Commentary of the Forty*, the author mentioned that love embraces both the unbeliever and the Muslim. He wants for his brother, the unbeliever, what he wants for himself by his becoming Muslim. He wants his Muslim brother to remain in Islam. So it is recommended to make supplication for guidance for the unbeliever. Love in this sense means to desire good and benefit. The love which is meant is in the *dīn*, it is not mortal love. Human nature may, in fact, dislike someone else gaining a blessing, but man must then oppose his human nature and ask Allah for good for his brother, and want for his brother what he wants for himself.

Almighty says, *"Messengers, eat of the good things and act rightly!"* (23:52) and the Almighty says, *"O you who believe, eat of the good things We have provided for you."* (2:172) Then he mentioned a man who goes on a long journey, is dishevelled and dusty and he stretches his hands to heaven, saying, 'O Lord! O Lord!' when his food is *ḥarām*, his drink is *ḥarām*, his clothes are *ḥarām*, and his sustenance is *ḥarām*. How could such a man be responded to?"[1]

Muslim related it in his *Ṣaḥīḥ* collection.

9. The *ḥadīth:*

"Do not inflict injury nor repay one injury with another."[2]

Mālik and ad-Dāraquṭnī and a group of notable men related it with an uninterrupted chain of transmission. It is an excellent *ḥadīth.*

10. Tamīm ad-Dārī, may Allah be pleased with him, reported that the Prophet, may Allah bless him and grant him peace, said:

---

1. "How can he be responded to?" His body is filled with the *ḥarām*. This shows explicitly that *taqwā* is not outward. Not everyone you see who is dirty or who lives a rough life is a righteous person – he must be judged by the *Sharī'a*. If he then appears perfect. then this is truly a virtuous man and it does not matter if he wears fine, new clothes or rags. But if he is lacking in the balance, he is one of the wretched, even if he wears the clothes of the people of *taqwā* and scrupulousness. Some people adopt an ascetic mode in order to attract and trap the hearts of people as well as their property. Some people wear clothes to show the blessings of Allah while others wear clothes out of pride and conceit. All of it revolves around the first *ḥadīth*, "Indeed, actions are by intentions." But always the real gauge is in either the following of the *Sharī'a* or the lack of following it.

2. Both courses are criticised by the *Sharī'a* because the *Sharī'a* does not permit you to profit by injury done to someone else. This is indicated by the words of Allah: *"Repel the bad with something better and, if there is enmity between you and someone else, he will be like a bosom friend."* (41:34)

"The *dīn* is faithfulness."[1] We asked, "To whom?" He replied, "To Allah, His Messenger, the Imams of the Muslims, and their common people."

Muslim related it.

11. Abū Hurayra, may Allah be pleased with him, said that he heard the Prophet, may Allah bless him and grant him peace, say:

"Stay with what I have left you [without asking for more]. Those before you were destroyed by their excessive questioning[2] and their disagreeing with their Prophets."

Everyone agrees that is is sound.

12. Sahl ibn Sa'īd, may Allah be pleased with him, said:

"A man came to the Messenger of Allah, may Allah bless him and grant him peace, and said, 'Messenger of

1. Faithfulness to Allah is sincerity in worship, denying any partner associated with Allah, avoiding any deviation from the right way, disconnecting Allah from every kind of imperfection and fault as you perform acts of obedience and urge them on others, avoiding acts of rebellion and impeding others from doing them, and love for Allah and hate for Allah. Faithfulness to the Messenger consists in confirming him, believing in what he brought, spreading his Message, giving life to his *Sunna*, curbing innovation, taking on his character, taking on his behaviour (*adab*) and love for Allah and the Companions of the Prophet, may Allah bless him and grant him peace. Faithfulness to the Muslim Imams consists in their helping people to the Truth and aiding their obedience in it, commanding it, forbidding what is against it, reminding them of it, and teaching them whatever they omit of it out of negligence. It is not correct to exalt them by praising them.

2. He said "by their excessive questioning" because it is the cause of disputes and disagreements. What the Messenger, may Allah bless him and grant him peace, warned about has occurred. There have been a number of question and many fantasies – highly improbable ones – written down in books which are studied and analysed. They are often about things which cannot normally occur. For instance, there is one that says, "If a bull mates with a cow and then gives birth to a man...." We can actually read this. Furthermore, it goes on to say that in this case it is permissible to slaughter the offspring on the day of the *'Īd*!

Allah, show me an action which will make Allah love me and people love me if I do it.' He replied, 'Do without with respect to this world[1] and Allah will love you. Do without with respect to what people have, and people will love you!"

It is an excellent *ḥadīth*. Ibn Mājah related it.

13. Ibn Mas'ūd, may Allah be pleased with him, reported that the Messenger of Allah, may Allah bless him and grant him peace, said:

"The blood of a Muslim who says that there is no god except Allah and that I am the Messenger of Allah is not lawful (to shed) except in three cases: a married man who commits adultery, a life for a life, and someone who abandons the dīn and splits up the community."

It is agreed to be sound.

14. 'Abdullāh ibn 'Umar, may Allah be pleased with him, reported that the Messenger of Allah, may Allah bless him and grant him peace, said:

"I am commanded to fight people until they testify that there is no god except Allah and Muhammad is the Messenger of Allah, establish the prayer, and pay the *zakāt*. If they do that, their lives and their property are

1. He said, "Do without in this world." He does not mean to abandon all activity and to withdraw from the world and be satisfied with living like a wild animal so that you become dependent on charity from others. That is disliked and undesirable. The Prophet, may Allah bless him and grant him peace, means to remove the love of this world from the heart while carrying out the obligatory duties. A Muslim should be neither tight-fisted nor extravagant. Allah has praised the one with economy and balance in His Book, saying, *"Those who, when they spend, are neither extravagant nor mean, but take a stance mid way between the two."* (25:67)

> protected from me, except for the right of Islam.[1] Their reckoning is up to Allah Almighty."

It is agreed that it is sound.

15. Ibn 'Umar, may Allah be pleased with him, reported that the Messenger of Allah, may Allah bless him and grant him peace, said:

> "Islam is based on five things: the testimony that there is no god except Allah and that Muhammad is the Messenger of Allah, performing the prayer, paying the *zakāt*-tax, performing the *ḥajj* to the House and fasting Ramaḍān."

It is agreed that it is sound.

---

1. "Except for the right of Islam and their reckoning is up to Allah," i.e. whoever abandons one of the rights of Islam has no right to protection. The command refers to shedding blood if there is harm in it for the Muslims. What is hidden in the conscience and heart is of no consequence. Allah will reckon that.

As for the question of the hypocrites and the fact that the Prophet did not kill any of them, their state did not reach the point where they displayed their true nature. That which they said to their brothers required fine interpretation to show their attack and hypocrisy. That is why Allah said, *"you will know them by their ambivalent speech."* (47:30) Ambivalent speech is a riddle or code which companions use so that no stranger will understand what they say. The poet said:

> I have used incorrect Arabic to you so that you will understand.
> Those who are intelligent understand ambivalent language.

When they wanted to consolidate their group, they built the Mosque of Harm. Allah seized them and commanded His Messenger to destroy their mosque. They were not helped by their ruse of the mosque being something outwardly desirable for the Muslims. The right of Islam demands that Islam be protected and not weakened. Supplication and claiming to love good is not helpful on its own. Had the people of the Mosque of Ḥarm been inside it, it would have been pulled down on top of them. However, they fled and their claim of sincerity did not preserve their mosque which was not for Allah. The real goal is to benefit Islam and the Muslims in every matter, form, state and place.

16. Ibn 'Abbās, may Allah be pleased with him, reported that the Messenger of Allah, may Allah bless him and grant him peace, said:

> "If people had been given everything they laid claim to, men would lay claim to the property of the people and their blood. However, the one making the claim must bring a clear proof, and the one who denies it must take an oath."

This *ḥadīth* is related in this way, while part of it is included in the *Ṣaḥīḥ* collections.

17. Wābiṣa ibn Ma'bad, may Allah be pleased with him, mentioned that he went to the Messenger of Allah, may Allah bless him and grant him peace, who said:

> "Have you come to ask me about piety (*birr*)?" "Yes," Wābiṣa replied. The Prophet said, "Consult your heart. Piety is that with which the soul is at rest and the heart is at rest. Wrong action is that about which you brood, and it echoes to and fro in your breast, even if people give a decision in your favour and ask for your opinion."

One version has, "even if the one asked gives a decision in your favour." It is an excellent *ḥadīth*. Aḥmad ibn Ḥanbal, ad-Dārimī and others have related it. The version of an-Nawwās ibn Sam'ān is in the *Ṣaḥīḥ* Collection of Muslim. He said, "Piety consists of good character and wrong action is that which you brood about in yourself and which you hate to show to people."

18. Shaddād ibn Aws, may Allah be pleased with him, reported that the Messenger of Allah, may Allah bless him and grant him peace, said:

> "Allah has prescribed excellent behaviour *(iḥsān)* for everything. Therefore when you kill, kill well. When you sacrifice, sacrifice well. Each of you should sharpen the edge of his knife and should calm down his sacrificial animal."

Muslim related it.

19. Abū Hurayra, may Allah be pleased with him, reported that the Messenger of Allah, may Allah bless him and grant him peace, said:

> "Whoever believes in Allah and the Last Day should speak what is good or remain silent.[1] Whoever believes in Allah and the Last Day should honour his neighbour. Whoever believe Allah and the Last Day should honour the guest."

It is agreed to be sound.

20. Abū Hurayra, may Allah be pleased with him, reported that a man said to the Prophet, may Allah bless him and grant him peace:

---

1. He said, "Let him speak what is good or remain silent." Ash-Shāfi'ī said that this *ḥadīth* means that when you want to speak, you should reflect. If it seems to you that there is harm in it, then hold back. For that reason, al-Qushayrī said, "Silence at the proper time is the attribute of men as speech at the proper time is one of the noblest of qualities." Ad-Daqqāq said, "Whoever is silent about the truth is a dumb *shayṭān*." He said that he should honour his neighbour. That is because mutual recognition begins with your neighbour whom Allah has recommended in the Book, *"and the near neighbour."* (4:36) To ignore your neighbour and honour someone else indicates that the honouring is deceit or an intention which is not good which occasions doubt. Honouring your neighbour precedes honouring others. When the person is accustomed to honour those near him, he does not refrain from honouring distant people. "Every man has what he falls back on in his life." A person is generous to his neighbour, so generosity is universal. "Let him honour his guest."

> "Give me some advice!" He said, "Do not get angry."[1] He repeated his request several times, and the Prophet said, "Do not get angry."

Al-Bukhārī related it in his *Ṣaḥīḥ* collection.

21. Abū Tha'laba, may Allah be pleased with him, reported that the Messenger of Allah, may Allah bless him and grant him peace, said:

> "Allah has has made certain things into obligations, so you should not neglect them! He has made certain things unlawful, so you should not commit them! He has been silent about certain things as a mercy to you without any forgetfulness on His part, so do not delve into them!"

Ad-Dāraquṭnī related it with an excellent chain of transmission.

22. Abū Dharr and Mu'ādh, may Allah be pleased with them, reported that the Messenger of Allah, may Allah bless him and grant him peace, said,

---

1. He said, "Do not get angry." Anger is a type of madness. It issues from man when he is vain and something does not please him. In that moment, he destroys what he has built up for many years because it is easier to destroy than it is to build. The goal of the Prophet, may Allah bless him and grant him peace, was to preserve sound actions. He urged them by repeating the advice when he said, "Do not get angry." He wanted to make it easy to remember what he meant by actions. If you threaten your actions with extinction, you cannot preserve anything. You will be like the one who amasses a lot of wealth and then throws it into the sea after a time and is content with that. The Prophet wants you to be in control of your intellect and feelings in all states and to preserve the good actions you have acquired in this life.

2. "Wherever you are." There is no difference between your secrets and what you make public. This is to direct you to sincerity because Allah is aware of you and what you hide is not hidden from Him. Your worship at home should not be less than your worship in the Masjid al-Ḥaram, with no difference between your actions. We do not make any difference between the times when people are present and when they are absent.

> "Fear Allah wherever you are.[2] Follow up an evil action with a good action which will wipe it out. Treat people well."[1]

At-Tirmidhī related it and said that it is an excellent *ḥadīth.* In some copies, he says that it is a sound/excellent *ḥadīth.*

23. Mu'ādh, may Allah be pleased with him, narrated:

> "I said, 'Messenger of Allah, tell me of an action I can do which will admit me to the Garden and keep me far away from the Fire!' He said, 'You have asked about a great matter, but it is easy for the one to whom Allah makes it easy. You should worship Allah and not associate anything with Him, do the prayer, pay the *zakāt*, fast Ramaḍān and go on *ḥajj* to the House.' Then the Prophet said, 'Shall I direct you to the gates of good? Fasting, which is protection, and *ṣadaqa*, which extinguishes mistakes as water extinguishes fire, and the prayer of a man in the middle of the night.' Then he recited, *'Their sides eschew their beds as they call on their Lord in fear and ardent hope. And they giveof what We have provided for them. No self knows the delight that is hidden away for it in recompense for what it used to do.'* (32:16-17) Then he said, 'Shall I tell you of the head of the matter, its support and its peak?' I said, 'Yes indeed, Messenger of Allah.' He

1. "Follow up an evil action with a good action which will wipe it out." Allah says, *"Good actions eradicate bad actionss."* (11:114) "Treat people well" because it is the fountain of virtues. Allah praised His Messenger Muḥammad for this excellent quality: *"Indeed you are truly vast in character."* (68:4) The *sunna* of Allah in His creation is to make people need each other. They cannot do without mutual help. Bad character seeks loneliness and a life apart from people. This is contrary to the teachings of the Islamic *dīn* which establishes gathering for prayer five times a day. How would one whose nature is incompatible with the nature of others be able to mix with them? When dissension and strife is about to occur, the Prophet, may Allah bless him and grant him peace, commanded people to have good character in order to be able to join forces.

said, 'The head of the matter is Islam and its support is the prayer and its peak is *jihād*.'[1] Then he said, 'Shall I tell you of the foundation of all that?' I said. 'Yes, Messenger of Allah.' He took hold of his tongue and said, 'Restrain this!' I said, 'Messenger of Allah, will we be taken to task for what we say?' He said, 'May your mother be bereaved! Are people thrown on their faces in the Fire for anything other but the harvest of their tongues?'"[2]

At-Tirmidhī related it and said that it is sound/excellent.

24. 'Irbād ibn Sārīya, may Allah be pleased with him, said:

"The Messenger of Allah, may Allah bless him and grant him peace, gave us a profound exhortation which made our hearts afraid and our eyes weep. We said, 'Messenger of Allah, it is an exhortation which is as if it were bidding us farewell, so advise us!' He said, 'I commend you to fear Allah and to hear and obey, even if a slave is put in command over you. Any among you who live long enough will see much disagreement, so you must hold to my Sunna and the sunna of the right-

1.The head of the matter and its support is *jihād*. That is because it demonstrates strength and might. This preserves security. Judgements are given when there is security. Allah is worshipped openly without any opposition or dissent. Abandoning *jihād* indicates weakness and submission to the enemy. Without it Islam would remain a house without a foundation.

2. How sweet is this sentence which the Prophet said! He said, "restrain this" because the tongue translates what is in the heart. A man can say what he does not believe and act in accordance with what he said. Offering excuses will not help you. Even if it helps you when the *ḥadd*-punishment is not carried out, it will not remove you from the doubt which you have started. You will not know how to free yourself from it. He said, "the harvest of tongues" because Allah has given man a great gift. It is that he is not to be punished for what the heart imagines and for a plan on its own. When he speaks, however, it is written down against him and he becomes accoutable for it. If it had not been for his tongue, he would have been innocent and safe.

ly-guided khalifs. Hold onto it with your teeth. Beware of new matters. Every innovation is misguidance.'"

Abū Dāwūd and at-Tirmidhī related it and said that it is a sound/excellent *ḥadīth.*

25. Ibn 'Abbās, may Allah be pleased with him, said:

"I was behind the Prophet, may Allah bless him and grant him peace, one day. He said, 'Young man, I will teach you some words. Hold fast to Allah and He will preserve you! Cling to Allah and you will find Him before you! If you ask, ask Allah.[1] If you seek help, seek it from Allah.[2] Know that even if the community were to join together to do something to benefit you, they could only benefit in what Allah has written for you. And if they were to join together to do something to harm you, they could only harm you in what Allah has written for you. The pens have been lifted and the pages are dry."

At-Tirmidhī related it, and said that it is a sound/excellent *ḥadīth.* In a variant other than the one of at-Tirmidhī, it says, "Hold fast to Allah and you will find Him before you! Recognise Allah in ease, and He will recognise you in hardship. Know that what has missed you could not have have come to you, and that what come to you could not have missed you!" Another version has, "Know that victory comes with steadfastness,[3] relief with trouble and ease with hardship."

---

1. He said to ask Allah because the might of Islam rejects abasement and humbleness to other than the Creator who has favour. Asking someone like you will lead you to apathy and consideration for the people you ask. Elevating humans is contrary to pure *tawḥīd.*

2. He said to ask Allah for help in respect to belief of harm and benefit, not for help in actions. Allah urged that, "Help each other to goodness and *taqwā.*" (5:2)

3. He said, "Victory comes with steadfastness." This is one of the principles

26. The *ḥadīth* of Ibn 'Umar from his father 'Umar ibn al-Khaṭṭāb:

"One day while we were sitting with the Messenger of Allah there appeared before us a man whose clothes were exceedingly white and whose hair was exceedingly black. No trace of travel could be seen on him and none of us knew him. He walked up and sat down by the Prophet. Resting his knees against his and placing the palms of his hands on his thighs, he said, 'O Muḥammad! Tell me about Islam.' The Messenger of Allah said, 'Islam is to testify that there is no god but Allah and that Muḥammad is the Messenger of Allah, to perform the prayers, to pay the *zakāt*, to fast in Ramaḍan and to make the pilgrimage to the House if you are able to do so.' He said, 'You have spoken the truth,' and we were amazed at him asking him and then saying that he had spoken the truth. He said, 'Then tell me about belief.' He said, 'It is to believe in Allah, His angels, His Books, His Messengers, and the Last Day, and to believe in the decree, both its good and its evil.' He said, 'You have spoken the truth.' He said, 'Then tell me about *iḥṣān*.' He said, 'It is to worship Allah as though you could see Him for while you do not see Him, He sees you.' He said, 'Then tell me about the Hour.' He said, 'The one asked about it knows no more about it than the asker.' He said, 'Then tell me about its signs.' He said, 'That a slavegirl will give birth to her mistress and that you will see barefooted, destitute herdsmen competing in constructing lofty buildings.'

---

of the *dīn*. Most people forget it. It is not giving any scope for despair to reach the heart. The Muslims must have strong resolution in the state of trouble no less than they have in the state of joy, and in the state of defeat no more than in the time of victory. They should direct their attention to *"We will certanly help Our Messengers and those who believe"* (40:51) and *"Truly it is the Party of Allah who are the successful."* (58:22)

> Then he left but I stayed on a while. Then the Prophet said, "Umar, do you know who the questioner was?' I said, 'Allah and His Messenger know best.' He said, 'It was Jibrīl who came to teach you your religion.'"

These are the *hadiths* which Shaykh Abū 'Amr ibn aṣ-Ṣalāḥ mentioned, may Allah have mercy on him. One *ḥadīth* with the same meaning is:

27. Sufyān ibn 'Abdullāh, may Allah be pleased with him, reported:

> "I said, 'Messenger of Allah, tell me something about Islam which I could not ask from anyone but you!' He said, 'Say, "I have believed in Allah," and then go straight.'"

Muslim related it.

28. Abu Mas'ūd 'Uqba ibn 'Amr al-Badrī, may Allah be pleased with him, reported:

> "The Prophet, may Allah bless him and grant him peace, said, "Provided it does not cause you shame,[1] do whatever you wish!"

Al-Bukhārī related it in his *Ṣaḥīḥ* collection.

29. Jābir, may Allah be pleased with him, reported that a man asked the Prophet, may Allah bless him and grant him peace:

---

1. He said, "Provided it does not cause you shame," i.e. before Allah and His Messenger, do not be worried about doing whatever you like. This is a warning. If you are travelling to Us and you will see the actions which you did. "Even if something weighs as little asa mustard-grain and is inside a rock or anywhere else in the heavens or earth, Allah will bring it out." (31:16)

"Do you think that if I pray the prescribed prayers, fast Ramaḍan, make *ḥalāl* what is *ḥalāl* and make *ḥarām* what is *ḥarām*, and do not do anything more than that, that I will enter the Garden?" He said, "Yes."

Muslim related it.

Chapter 2

The Reality of Sincerity (*Ikhlāṣ*) and Truthfulness (*Ṣidq*)

As far as sincerity (*ikhlāṣ*) is concerned, Allah Almighty says:

> *"They were only ordered to worship Allah, making their* dīn *sincerely His."* (98:5)

Ḥudhayfa ibn an-Nu'mān, may Allah be pleased with him, said, "I asked the Messenger of Allah, may Allah bless him and grant him peace, what sincerity is. He replied, 'I asked Jibrīl about sincerity and he answered, "I asked the Lord of Might about sincerity and He said, 'It is one of My secrets which I place in the heart of whichever of My slaves I love.'"'"

Al-Qushayri said, "Sincerity is to make Allah alone your intention in obedience. It is that you mean to draw near to Allah by obedience. It is nothing else, not hypocrisy for the sake of a creature, nor earning the praise of people nor an act demanding praise from creation nor anything else other than drawing near to Allah Almighty!"

He also said, "It would be valid to call sincerity being on your guard against any consideration for other people."

Abū 'Alī ad-Daqqāq stated, "Sincerity is being on your guard against considering creatures, truthfulness, and continuing to read the self (*nafs*). The sincere person does not show off, and the true man is not vain."

Dhū'n-Nūn al-Miṣrī said, "Sincerity has three signs: praise and blame from common people are the same for you; you forget to see actions when you act; and the reward of the action is paid to you in the Next World."

Abū 'Uthmān al-Maghribī observed: "Sincerity is forgetting to see creation by constantly looking at the Creator."

Hudhayfa al-Mar'ashī said, "Sincerity is that the inward and outward actions of the slave are the same."

Fuḍayl ibn 'Iyāḍ said, "To refrain from an action for the sake of people is showing-off. To act for the sake of people is associating partners with Allah in idolatry. Sincerity is that Allah frees you of from both considerations."

Sahl ibn 'Abdullāh at-Tustarī was asked, "What is stronger than the self?" He replied, "Sincerity, since it is something the self has no share in."

Yūsuf ibn al-Ḥusayn stated, "The greatest thing in this world is sincerity!"

Abū 'Uthmān al-Maghribī said, "The sincerity of the common people is that which the self has no share in. The sincerity of the elite is what is bestowed on them – it does not happen by them. Acts of obedience appear from them while they are cut off from them, and they do not see them nor reckon them."

Makḥūl said, "When a slave is sincere for forty days, the springs of wisdom must appear on his tongue from his heart."

Sahl at-Tustarī said, "If anyone goes without (*zuhd*) this world for forty days with truthfulness in his heart and sincerity, miracles (*karāmāt*) will appear from him. If no miracles appear from him, that is due to lack of true sincerity in his doing-without." Someone asked Sahl, "How are the miracles manifested?" He said, "He takes whatever he likes from wherever he likes."

Sahl at-Tustari also said, "Shrewd men look into the obsprac-tice ervation of sincerity and discover only that its movement and its stillness, its secrecy and its openness are for Allah alone. Nothing is mixed with it, neither the self, nor emotions, nor this world."

As-Sari as-Saqaṭī said, "Do not do anything for people nor leave anything for them! Do not give anything to them, and do not unveil anything to them!"

As for truthfulness (*ṣidq*), Allah says:

> *"O who you believe! Have fear of Allah* (taqwā) *and be with the truthful."* (9:120)[1]

Al-Qushayrī noted, "Truthfulness is the basis of the matter and it is made perfect by it, and it is commanded." He said, "The least truthfulness is when what is secret and what is public are the same."

Sahl said, "The scent of truthfulness has not been smelt by any person who flatters either himself or another person."

"Truthfulness is the sword of Allah," said Dhū'n-Nūn al-Miṣrī. "It is not applied to anything but that it cuts right through it."

Al-Ḥārith al-Muḥāsibī said, "The truthful man is the one who does not care if his entire worth in the hearts of men should vanish away if it is for the sake of putting his heart in harmony. He does not like people to know about his least good action, and he does not dislike people being be aware of his bad actions. If he does dislike that, it is proof that he desires to be greater in their eyes. This is not the sincerity of the truthful ones."

It is said that if you seek truthfulness from Allah, He will give you a mirror in which you can see the baseless falsehood of this world and the Next.

The master, Abū'l-Qāsim al-Junayd, said, "The truthful man is turned about forty times a day, while the show-off is fixed in the same state for forty years."

---

1. "Be among the truthful" because the one who sits with someone is influenced for good and evil. Nature is a thief. A man copies the one he mixes with a lot, even if he is not aware of it. Ṭarafa said,

> Do not ask about a man. Ask about his close companions.
> Every man imitates his close companions.

This is the best path to travel for someone who wants to discipline himself. It is to mix with the perfect man so that his nature and good habits flow to him. The influence of actions is absolutely stronger than the influence of words.

By this, he means that the truthful man changes direction with the truth, no matter what it is. When sees something in the *Sharī'a* which is considered to be excellent, he promptly does it, even if it is at variance with his customary habit. If something arises in the *Sharī'a* which is more important, but he cannot combine the two things, then he moves to the better one. He continues to behave like that. In a single day, he may have a hundred different states, or a thousand or even more, according to his mastery of gnosis, and the manifestation to him of fine points and subtleties.

The show-off, on the other hand, clings to one state alone, and if something arises which the *Sharī'a* considers more important in some states, then he will still not do that important thing. He will hold fast to his state, because he is showing off his worship and his state to creation. He fears that people will stop loving him if he changes. He is very careful to insure that their love continues. But the truthful one desires only the Face of Allah by his worship. Whenever the *Sharī'a* gives greater weight to a certain state, he goes to that state, and does not turn to creation.

Chapter 3

The Importance of Intention

Know that when you desire to perform any act of obedience, no matter how small, you must have a conscious intention. That means that you intend to please Allah by your action. Your intention should be simultaneous with the action. This includes all acts of worship: the prayer, fasting, *wuḍū'*, *tayammum*, retreat, *ḥajj*, paying the *zakāt*, giving charity, taking care of needs, visiting the sick, following a funeral, initiating the greeting and returning it, blessing anyone who sneezes, objecting to what is rejected as wrong, and commanding what is recognised as right, answering an invitation, attending gatherings of knowledge and *dhikr*, visiting virtuous people, spending on your family and guests, honouring the people you love and close relatives, learning knowledge and discussing it, repeating it, teaching it, instructing in it, reading it, writing it and putting it in order, giving legal opinions (*fatwās*), and any other similar actions. It is applicable to such an extent that you should make an intention when you eat, drink, or go to sleep. By doing this, you intend fearful awareness in obedience to Allah, or to give the body a rest in order to have more energy for obeying Allah. It is the same when you want to have sexual intercourse with your wife. You intend by it to give her the rights due to her, to obtain a good child who will worship Allah, and to refrain from looking at what is *ḥarām* and dwelling on it and to protect yourself from it.

Whoever lacks an intention in these actions is denied great good. Whoever is successful in making one has been given a vast favour. We ask Allah the Generous for success in this matter and in all aspects of good. The proof of this principle is contained in the words of the Prophet, may Allah bless him and grant him peace,

"Indeed, actions are according to intentions, and every man has what he intends!"

They say that someone said to Ḥabīb ibn 'Abī Thābit at-Tābi'ī, the *muftī* of the people of Kūfa and a very reliable man, "Tell us about the most difficult thing to do!" He replied, "To have a conscious intention!"

Sufyān ath-Thawrī stated, "I have do not have to deal with anything more difficult for me than my intention."[1]

Yazīd ibn Hārūn said, "The only reason intention is so exalted in the *ḥadith* is because of its nobility."

Ibn 'Abbās stated, "Man is protected according to his intention."

Muḥammad ibn Idrīs ash-Shāfi'ī said, "I would like people to learn this, even though not one single letter of it is ascribed to me."

Ash-Shāfi'ī also said, "I have never competed with anyone with the idea of defeating him. Whenever I compete with anyone, it is only in order to show him the truth."

He also said, "I have never spoken to anyone without wanting success for him, and desiring that he be directed to the right way, be helped and have protection and preservation from Allah Almighty."

Abū Yūsuf, Abū Ḥanīfa's disciple, stated, "I desire to teach you for the sake of Allah. I never sit down in any assembly in which I intend to be humble without standing up having elevated them. And I do not sit down in any assembly in which I intend to elevate them without standing up having been compromised."

1. He means sincerity and purifying actions of impurities which tarnish the action or postpone it. He strives to make his action sincere and purely for Allah. Had he simply meant intention as goal, that would be terribly easy. If you are exact in what the *Salaf* discussed, they helped one another through difficulties in order to make the intention correct. The reason for that is that they wanted their actions to be free of any defect to win acceptance from Allah.

Chapter 4

It states in a sound *ḥadīth* that the Messenger of Allah, may Allah bless him and grant him peace, said, "Allah Almighty records both good actions and bad actions. If anyone intends to perform a good action and does not do it, Allah records a completed good action for him. If he intends to do it, and then actually does do it, Allah writes down ten good actions for him, or seven hundred, or many more."

We find in the *Ṣaḥīḥ* Collection that the Messenger of Allah, may Allah bless him and grant him peace, remarked about the army which will advance against the Ka'ba, "They will be swallowed up by the earth, the first and the last of them." 'Ā'isha asked, "Messenger of Allah, why will all of them be swallowed up, the first and the last, when traders are among them and others who are not actually a part of them?" He replied, "They will be swallowed up, the first and the last, and then they will be resurrected according to their intentions."

It is reported in the two *Ṣaḥīḥ* collections that Ibn 'Abbās said, "There is no emigration (*hijra*) after the Victory of Makka, but there is struggling in *jihād* and there is intention."

Our companions and other scholars have disagreed about the meaning of "There is no emigration after the Victory of Makka." It has been said that it means that there is no emigration from Makka since now it is the Abode of Islam. It is also said that no emigration after the blessing of the victory has been achieved. As for emigration from the abode of the unbelievers today, it is absolutely confirmed that it is obligatory for someone who is in a position to do so if he cannot proclaim the *dīn* of Islam there. If he can, then it is recommended, but not obligatory. Allah knows best.

'Amr ibn Shuraḥbīl al-Hamdānī took a gift he had been given in order to give out some *ṣadaqa* from it. When he returned to his family and counted what was left, he found that it remained at exactly the same amount as before. He said to his nephew, "Why do you not do the same as this?" His nephew replied, "If we knew it would not get smaller, we would do it." "Umar said, "I do not set conditions for my Lord, the Mighty, the Majestic!"

Our Imam, Muḥammad ibn Idrīs ash-Shāfi'ī, said, "The good of this world and the Next World lies in five qualities: the independence of the self, restraint from harm, gaining what is lawful, the safeguard of fear of Allah, and reliance on Allah Almighty in every state."

Ḥammād ibn Salama, who was thought to be one of the *abdāl*, said, "Whoever utters a *ḥadīth* for other-than-Allah is deceived by it."[1]

Aḥmad ibn Abī'l-Ḥawārī wrote the *Book of Zuhd* and later I will relate some passages from it, Allah willing. Its chain of transmission does not extend up to the present day, but I have an excellent, accurate copy of it. One of the people of knowledge and experience told me that the handwriting is that of ad-Dāraquṭnī. Aḥmad said, "I had it from Isḥāq ibn Khālid, who had it from Ḥafṣ ibn Ghiyāth that 'Abdu'r-Raḥmān ibn al-Aswad said, "You should never eat bread without an intention." I asked Isḥāq, "What is the intention in eating bread?" He replied, "If someone is too sluggish to do the prayer, it makes him more energetic and so he eats bread in order to become more agile. If he is too light or too weak, then he eats it in order to give himself strength. His eating it and his avoiding it are for the prayer." By becoming more agile, that person means to become energetic so that he may find ease and enjoyment in the prayer.

1. He says that it deceives him because knowledge is like a ferocious lion. *Ḥadīth* is the core of knowledge. It is called the attacking lion among the wild beasts. This lion can only be overcome through the help of Allah. A man must prepare for it to reach him by having *taqwā* of Allah and making his intention sincere so that he can ride the lion or place it under his power and authority. Even if he overcomes the lion, he must be alert and completely on his guard because if you neglect a lion, it will become unsubmissive. Then it will attack its owner and kill him. This is what Ḥammād ibn Salama meant when he said that the *ḥadīth* can deceive the one who seeks it for other than Allah.

Aḥmad ibn Abī'l-Ḥawārī also said, "I heard Abū Sulayman ad-Dārānī say, 'When you deal with Allah, deal with your hearts!' He means that you must purify your hearts, clean them and discipline them, and you must not neglect any of the outward actions. Abū Sulaymān was one of the great gnostics. He had miracles, splendid states, and excellent aphorisms. His name was 'Abdu'r-Raḥmān ibn Aḥmad. If Allah wills, I will transmit some gems about him. He was one of the later men in our city, Damascus. He said, "None of you will understand what it is you have obtained if you think it comes by means of a great deal of prayer and fasting. It is by the nobility of the self,[1] soundness of the heart and good counsel for the community."

Imām ash-Shāfi'ī said, "Whoever wants Allah to give him good must have a good opinion of people."

Shaykh Abū'l-Baqā' spoke to us one day while he were studying with him. He said that he heard 'Abdu'l-Ghanī relate with an *isnād* going back to Abū Qubaysa, who saw Sufyān ath-Thawrī in a dream. He asked him, "What has Allah done with you?" He answered:

I looked at my Lord face-to-face.
He said to me, "Enjoy My pleasure with you, Ibn Sa'īd!

---

1 "By the nobility of the self." That is because the prayer encourages man to do pleasing actions and to avoid censured actions. Allah says, *"The prayer precludes indecency and wrongdoing."* (29:45) Nobility of the self is only combined with the prayer. It would not occur to you that someone who abandons the prayer would have good counsel, generosity, and a sound heart. It is confirmed that when someone does that, it is to deceive people and to influence their intellects and their property. Or such people might simply desire praise and commendation. If he had desired the face of Allah by his action, it would have been obedience. So it is up to you. Allah says, *"The prayer is prescribed for the believers at specific times."* (4:103) A man's action is either for the sake of Allah – and if he claims that while he has abandoned the prayer, he is a liar because you do not reach the will of Allah by rebellion against Allah – or it is for people. This is not nobility. He is like a hunter who puts out food to trap game. If he does not desire the *dīn* or this world, that is a tool of subjugation, and such an action cannot be described with praise or commendation. There is no doubt that he means that much prayer is what is not for the sake of that because prayer is the foundation of virtues and the degrees by which a person rises to perfection both in this world and the Next.

> When the darkness was very great, you went straight
> with longing, good counsel and an intent heart.
>
> Here you are! Choose any castle you desire!
> Visit Me, for I am not far from you!"

"I looked at my Lord face-to-face" means that he had eye-witnessing without either veil or messenger. "When the darkness was very great" means intense darkness. He said "intent", which means he is a lover with sincere love for Allah. The linguists say that "an intent heart" is possessed by someone whom passionate love shakes violently.

Shaykh Abū'l-Baqā' related with an *isnād* that Yaḥyā ibn Mu'ādh ar-Rāzī remarked, "How many a one who asks forgiveness is hated, and how many a one who is silent is shown mercy! One man asks forgiveness while his heart remains shameless and another man remains silent while his heart is in remembrance!"

Abū'l-Ḥasan al-Wā'ī heard Aḥmad ibn 'Aṭā ar-Rūdhbārī say, "Whoever goes out to seek knowledge wanting to use it for his own benefit obtains only a little."

He also said, "Knowledge is dependent upon acting on it." He means by that the useful knowledge which is sought after. It is just as Imām ash-Shāfi'ī said, "Knowledge is not what is memorised. Knowledge is what benefits."

Our shaykh, Abū'l-Baqā', reported that Qāsim al-Jū'ī said, "The *dīn* is scrupulousness. The best worship is passing the night in prayer. The best path to the Garden is the soundness of the heart."

Abū Sa'īd as-Sam'ānī said in the *Book of Lineages*, "This Qāsim al-Jū'ī had miracles which were related to hunger (*jū'*). He often went hungry."

Shaykh Abū'l-Baqā' related to us that Abū Bakr ad-Duqqī heard Abū Bakr az-Zaqqāq say, "This matter is of ours is built on four things: we only eat when we need to, we only sleep when we are overcome with fatigue. we are only silent out of fear,[1] and we only speak from ecstasy."

Ad-Duqqī is one of the great Sufis and people of gnosis and miracles. He died in 260 AH. As for az-Zaqqāq, as-Sam'ānī said that his name is derived from skins (*ziqq*) which he worked with and sold. Abū Bakr az-Zaqqāq was one of the great Sufis with outward miracles and evident gnosis.

Az-Zaqqāq also said, "Everyone is related to some lineage with the exception of the needy (*fuqarā'*) They are are related to Allah Almighty. Every reckoning and lineage is cut off except for their reckoning. Their lineage is truthfulness and their reckoning is poverty."

Al-Bayhaqī reported that Imām ash-Shāfi'ī said, "Abū Mūsā, if you were to strive with all your might to please everyone, you still could never accomplish it. Since that is the way things are, make your action and your intention sincere for Allah."

Shaykh Abū'l-Baqā' reported that Abū 'Abdullāh 'Uthmān al-Maghribī said, "A man who shovels mud is better than a Sufi without truthfulness."

Several people report that Muqātal ibn Ṣāliḥ al-Khurāsānī said, "I went to see Ḥammād ibn Salama. There was nothing in his house except the mat he was sitting on, a Qur'ān he was reading, a bag which contained his knowledge, and a jug from which he did *wuḍū'*. While I was with him, there was a knock at the door. He said, 'Girl, go and see who it is.' She came back and said, 'It is a messenger from Muḥammad ibn Sulaymān.' He said, 'Tell him to come in.' He came in, greeted him, and then gave him a letter. The messenger said, 'Read this.' It said, 'In the name of Allah, the All-Merciful, Most Merciful, from Muḥammad ibn Sulaymān to

1. He said, "out of fear." When he begins to speak he is not concerned about the wrath or pleasure of the one he addresses. He speaks the truth openly and is only silent when he fears that the one he addresses will be misguided or will swerve aside, or he fears that he himself will be overcome by showing-off and vanity. In such a case he will be afflicted by a worse sickness than the one he wants to heal in someone else. This is the meaning of fear lest a man deceive himself and be carried away by a string of words. He would be the sacrifice like the candle which gives light to others while it is burned up itself.

Ḥammād ibn Salama. May Allah give you what He has given His friends and the people of His obedience! A question has arisen and we wish to ask you about it.'

"Ḥammād said, 'Girl, bring me the inkwell!' Then he said, 'Now, write this on the back of the letter: "May He give you what He has give His friends and the people of His obedience. We know the scholars. They do not come to anyone. If a problem has arisen come to us and ask us about what seems right to you. If you come to us, only come to us alone. Do not come with your horse or your man, or I will not counsel either you or myself. Peace!"'

"Then while I was still sitting with him, there was another knock at the door. He said, 'Girl, go and see who it is!' She came back and said, 'It is Muḥammad ibn Sulaymān.' Ḥammād ordered, 'Tell him to come in alone.'

"When he came in, he greeted him and sat down before him. Muḥammad said, 'Why is it that when I look at you, I am filled with alarm?' Ḥammād replied, 'I heard someone who is reliable (and he meant al-Bunānī[1]) say, "I heard Anas ibn Mālik, may Allah be pleased with him, say, 'I heard the Messenger of Allah, may Allah bless him and grant him peace, say, "When the knower desires the face of Allah with his knowledge, everything stands in awe of him, but when he desires to increase his own treasuries by it, then he stands in awe of everything."'"'

"Muḥammad said, 'What do you think, may Allah have mercy on you, about a man who has two sons and is pleased with one of them and decides to give him two-thirds of his property while he is still alive?'

"Ḥammād said, 'I heard someone who is reliable, al-Bunānī, relate from Anas ibn Mālik, who heard the Messenger of Allah, may Allah bless him and grant him peace, say, "When Allah Almighty wants to punish a slave by means of what he has, he gives him success in bequeathing a permitted legacy when he dies."'"

"Muḥmmad said, 'One more thing...'

1. Meaning Thābit ibn Aslam al-Bunānī.

"Ḥammād said, 'Let's have it so long as it is not something harmful to the *dīn* of Allah.'

"Muḥammad said, '40,000 dirhams against what you are due...'

"Ḥammād replied, 'Return it to the one you have wronged by it!'

"Muḥammad insisted, 'By Allah, I only gave you what you inherited!'

"Ḥammād replied, 'I have no need of it.'

"Muḥammad said, 'Remove it from me, and Allah will remove your visitors from you.'

"Ḥammād said, 'Something else.'

"Muḥammad said, 'Let's have it so long as it is not something harmful to the *dīn* of Allah.'

"Ḥammād said, 'Take it and distribute it.'

"Muḥammad said, 'Even if I am equitable in distributing it, someone who receives no provision from it might say that I did not distribute it fairly! By that, he would be committing a wrong action. Remove it from me, and Allah will remove your visitors from you!'"

What an excellent story this is! How excellent are its benefits, and what gems and information about important rules are contained in it!

While I was studying with our Shaykh, Abū'l-Baqā', he related to me from in an *isnād* going back to Abū 'Abdullāh at-Tamīmī who reported that his father said, "I saw Ḥammād ibn Salama in a dream. I said, 'What has your Lord done with you?' He said, 'Good!' I said, 'What?' He said, 'He said to me, "How often you exhausted yourself! Today, I will make your rest long and I will make the rest of those who exhaust themselves for My sake long. How excellent is what I prepared for them!"'"

CHAPTER 5

Transmitted Gems

In the *Ṣaḥīḥ* Collection of al-Bukhārī it is reported that 'Ammār ibn Yasār said, "Whoever possesses three qualities possesses all belief: he gives other people what is due to them, gives the greeting to everyone, and spends [in the Cause of Allah] even when he is poor."

He has combined the good of this world and the Next World in these words. They indicate the essence of Islam. Whoever acts fairly in whatever he owes Allah and creation, and gives people good counsel and protection as much as he can, has achieved full obedience. He continued by saying, "giving the greeting to the everyone," i.e people in general. Being overbearing to people is to put oneself above them, The Prophet, may Prophet bless him and grant him peace, said, "Give the greeting to the one you know and to the one you do not know!"[1]

This is one of the greatest aspects of noble character. It ensults in security from enmity, rancour, belittling of people, being overbearing to them, and elevating oneself above them. Spending even when one is poor is the greatest possible generosity. Allah praised that, saying: *'They prefer them to themselves even if they themselves are needy."* (59:9) In general, this means spending on one's family, for the guest, the one who asks for something and every

1. This leads to mutual recognition which is one of the most important pillars of Islam and one of the greatest benefits of *ḥajj* which Allah mentions. The Prophet placed the benefits before remembrance to show his concern for it. Even if the "and" applies to the conjunction, it does not inform about advancing or delaying in respect to the Arabic language. There is the *ḥadīth* of Jābir which ad-Dāraquṭnī related in which the Prophet, may Allah bless him and grant him peace, said, "Begin with that with which Allah began." That indicates precedence and concern in action.

other expenditure in obedience to Allah Almighty. It ensures trust in Allah and reliance on the vastness of His bounty. Trust is the guarantee of provision. It also ensures doing-without in this world, not hoarding its goods, not being concerned with it, and not boasting and accumulating much of it.

Muslim says in his *Ṣaḥīḥ* collection, "Yaḥyā ibn Yaḥyā related to us from 'Abdullāh ibn Abī Yaḥyā ibn Abī Kathīr who said that he heard his father say, 'Knowledge is not possible when the body is at rest.'"

Al-Bukhāri reported in his *Ṣaḥīḥ* collection that Rabī'a said, "The person who has some knowledge should not waste himself [by abstaining from teaching it to others]."

The first of the two statements means that whoever has been given a rank in knowledge and acquires some of it while the tokens of its excellence appear to him must strive to complete it and not squander it. He would squander himself if he did not continue. The second statement means that whoever obtains knowledge must try to disseminate it and seek Allah's pleasure by it, and he must make it known to people by transmitting it so as to let both other people and himself benefit by it. He must be gentle in unfolding his knowledge to those who take it from him, and he must make the means to that easy in order to be more effective in giving good counsel. The *dīn* is good counsel.

The companions of ash-Shāfi'ī disagreed about the one who fits the first description. Is it a specific obligation for him to complete the search and is it unlawful for him to abandon it? Or does it remain an obligation in respect of him, even though it is not unlawful for him to abandon it if someone else undertakes it? This second opinion is the one most of them espoused. It is sound, and it is the best, but Allah knows best.

It is related from 'Umar ibn al-Khaṭṭāb and his son, 'Abdullāh: "Whoever is reticent makes his knowledge reticent." This means that whoever is shy in seeking knowledge obtains little knowledge.

Al-Bukhārī reported in his *Ṣaḥīḥ* Collection that Mujāhid said, "Neither a timid nor an arrogant one will learn knowledge."

Muslim and others have related that 'Ā'isha, may Allah be pleased with her, said, "The best women are the women of the Anṣār. Modesty does not prevent them from seeking understanding in the *dīn*."

Al-Bukhārī reported in his *Ṣaḥīḥ* Collection that 'Umar said, "Seek understanding before you have power." By that he meant that you should be intent on perfecting your knowledge and on being firm in acquiring it while you are young, still without occupation, leadership or age. When you are older and become leaders who are followed, then you will be prevented from seeking understanding and acquisition of knowledge. This is similar to ash-Shāfi'ī's words, "Seek understanding before you lead. When you lead, then there is no way to seek understanding."

Shaykh Abū'l-Baqā' related to us that Ja'far al-Khuldī heard al-Junayd state, "I do not look forward to dying since I am aware that I fear the earth will not accept me, and I will be exposed."

He also reported that al-Junayd mentioned that he heard Sarī as-Saqaṭī say. "I look at my nose twice a day out of the fear that my face will have turned black."

He further reported that 'Alī ibn al-Qāsim heard al-Ḥusayn ibn Kūjak say, "One of the best gifts is intellect and one of the worst afflictions is ignorance."

He also reported from Muḥammad ibn 'Abdullāh, the disciple of Bishr ibn al-Ḥārith, heard Ibn al-Ḥārith say, "They do not eat for pleasure nor dress in luxury." He added, "This is the path of the Next World, and the path of the Prophets and the righteous and whoever follows them. Whoever claims that the matter lies in something else is deceived."

He reported that Sahl ibn 'Abdullāh said, "It is unlawful for the heart to smell the scent of certainty while it relies on anything other-than-Allah! It is unlawful for light to enter a heart while there is something in it that Allah dislikes!"

He reported that Muḥammad ibn Nu'aym ibn Haysam heard Bishr ibn al-Ḥārith say, "Allah revealed by inspiration to Dā'ud, may Allah grant him peace, 'Dā'ud! Do not put a scholar who is deceived between you and Me, one who would block you from the path of My love by his bolting the door! Those are the ones who cut off the path of My slaves!' We ask Allah for well-being!"

Three of our shaykhs, Qāḍī Abū'l-Faḍl al-Anṣārī, Abū'l-Baqā' Yūsuf, and Shaykh Abū 'Abdulāh al-Anṣārī, all of them from Damascus, related to us that Salmān said, "People will not know how Allah helps the weak while they are not patient before that happens."

Ash-Shāfi'ī said, "You must have the quality of doing-without (*zuhd*). Doing-without for someone who does without is better than jewels on a young woman."

Ar-Rabī' reported that ash-Shāfi'ī said to him, "Rabi', do not talk about what does not concern you. If you talk about this world, it owns you and then you do not own it."

Al-Muzanī said, "I heard ash-Shāfi'ī say, 'No one can avoid having someone who hates him. Since this is unavoidable, a man should be with the people of obedience to Allah Almighty."

Al-Ḥasan ibn 'Imrān ibn 'Uyayna remarked that Sufyān ibn 'Uyayna said to him at Muzdalifa at the end of the *ḥajj*, "I have come to this place seventy times. Each time I say, 'O Allah, do not bring the contract to an end in this place!' I am too shy before the Mighty and Majestic, to ask Him for anything more than that." He came back and died within the year.

The trusty shaykh and master, Abū'l-Faḍl al-Bakrī spoke to us while we were studying with him at the Damascus mosque. He related to us that Aḥmad ibn Abī'l-Ḥawārī said, "I wanted to see Abū Sulaymān ad-Darānī in a dream. A year later I dreamt of him and asked, 'Teacher! What has Allah done with you?' He replied, 'Muḥammad, I once came out of the Bāb as-Saghīr and ran into the camel of a shaykh. I took a twig from it - I don't know whether I broke it or threw it away. I have been called to account for that for an entire year up to this very night!'" How profound this story is! It urges you to be scrupulous and to be on guard against being tolerant and indulgent with regard to seemingly insignificant wrong actions.

Our shaykh, Abū Isḥāq al-Murādī, spoke to me while I was studying with him. He related to me that Abū'l-'Abbās as-Sarrāj heard 'Abdullāh al-Warrāq say in the days of sedition while they were fighting, "Leave!" He used to say to them, "Leave, may Allah give you a good morning! Leave, may Allah give you blessing!" It is said that they abandoned the fighting. He said, "Allah has given them a good morning. They did not fight!"

Abū Isḥāq also related to us that as-Sarrāj said that Ibn Abī'd-Dunyā once sat down courteously. Then someone slandered another man. "You!" he exclaimed, "Listen! Remember a day when the earth will be put over your eyes!"

In the same chain of transmission, as-Sarrāj related from Yaḥyā ibn Abī Ṭālib from Ya'qūb, the nephew of Ma'rūf, who heard his uncle say, "Talking about what does not concern you makes Allah disappointed with you."

As-Sarrāj also heard 'Alī ibn al-Muwaffiq say that aart of Ma'rūf's supplication was, "O Master! O Powerful! There is nothing like You!"

He also reported that Khālid ibn Tamīm said that he saw Ibrāhīm ibn Adham in Syria. He asked him, "What has brought you here?" He replied, "I did not come here to struggle in *jihād* or enter a *ribāṭ*, but I came here to fill up on *ḥalāl* bread!"

Aḥmad al-'Ajali related that Rabī' at-Tābi'ī was a trustworthy man who never told a lie. He had two sons who rebelled during the governorship of al-Ḥajjāj. Al-Ḥajjāj was told, "Their father never tells a lie. Why don't you send a messenger to him to enquire about them?" He sent a messenger to him who asked, "Where are your sons?" He said, "In the house." He said, "We have pardoned them because of your truthfulness."

Al-Ḥārith al-Ghāzī told Ribi' ibn Khirāsh not to laugh until he knew his fate. He did not laugh until after he died. He had told Rabī' not to laugh until he knew whether he was in the Garden or the Fire. Al-Ḥārith said, "The man who washed him told him that he was still smiling on his bed while we were washing him until we were done."

Aḥmad ibn 'Abdullāh said, "The reciters of Kūfa gathered together in the house of the governor, Ibn 'Utayba, to study under Ṭalḥa ibn Muṣarrif. Word of that reached Ṭalḥa, so he went to sit with al-A'mash to study under him in order to remove that reputation from himself."

Imām ash-Shāfi'ī mentioned that someone said to Ubayy ibn Ka'b, "Abū'l-Mundhir, advise me!" He replied, "Be a brother to the brothers according to their fearful awareness of Allah.[1] Do not let your tongue begin to speak to someone who does not envy the living anything except that for which you envy the dead!"

Ash-Shāfi'ī mentioned that Fuḍayl ibn 'Iyāḍ said, "How many a person does *ṭawāf* of the Ka'ba, while someone else far away from it has a greater reward than he does."

Ash-Shāfi'ī also reported that the Prophet Dā'ud, peace be upon him, said, "My God! Be for my son as You have been for me!" Allah revealed by inspiration to him, "Dā'ud, tell your son to be for Me as you have been for Me! I will be for him as I have been for you!"

Ash-Shāfi'ī related that Hishām ibn 'Abdi'l-Mālik said, "Present your need to me!" He replied, "I have presented it to the Generous, the Noble."

In the "Chapter on the Miracles of the *Awliyā*'" in the *Risāla* of al-Qushayri he mentioned that Ja'far al-Khuldī had a stone. One day it fell into the Tigris River. He had a special supplication to entice lost objects to return. He recited that supplication and then found the stone in the middle of some leaves. Al-Qushayri said that Abū Hātim as-Sijistānī heard Abū Naṣr as-Sarrāj say, "That supplication was, 'O You who will gather mankind on the Day about which there is no doubt, gather my lost object to me!" I have tried this supplication myself and have found it to be a useful

1. He indicates the *āyat*, *"The believers are brothers,"* (19:10) i.e. in the *dīn*. The basis of the *dīn* is *taqwā*. Whenever it increases, the bonds of kinship are strengthened and connections in the *dīn* are consolidate. Someone acts according to his *taqwā* and is trusted. Someone who lacks it does not deserve to be treated as a brother. That understanding is strengthened by his words, "Do not let your tongue begin to speak..." You may speak to him and be a reason for injury to him. You may make his action desirable to him and make it seem good in his eyes while he should shun it. You have then become his partner in his action while nothing except the burden and error come back to you. No one envies a corpse and no one is enticed into arguing with it to do injustice to its rights. It should be like that with the living so that it will indicate your sincerity and *taqwā*.

means for quickly finding a lost object. The object does not run off. I heard my shaykh, Abū'l-Baqā', who was the first to teach it to me, say more or less the same thing.

Ja'far al-Khuldī al-Khawwāṣ was one of the Sufi shaykhs who had miracles. There is a story associated with how he came to be called al-Khuldī. Once he was with al-Junayd when he was asked a question. Al-Junayd turned and said to him, "Answer them!" He answered them and al-Junayd said, "How did you obtain these answers?" He said, "From my mole (*khuldī*)." So he kept that name. He died in 348 AH. Ad-Dāraquṭnī, Abū Ḥafs ibn Shāhīn and others have related sayings from him. He is trustworthy.

Al-Ḥārith ibn Usāma and others relate that Aḥmad ibn Abī'l-Ḥawārī said in the *Book of Zuhd*, "I heard one of our companions – and I think it was Abū Sulaymān ad-Dārānī – say, 'Iblīs has a *shayṭān* called Mutaqadī (litigant). He makes claims against the son of Adam for twenty years in order to make his secret actions public. He displays that to disclose the difference between what is secret and what is out in the open."[1]

Ibrāhīm ibn Sa'd said, "I asked Sa'd ibn Ibrāhīm, 'Why was az-Zuhrī above you?' He answered, 'Because he used to sit at the front of gatherings and did remain at the back. There was no young man in the gathering he did not question, or middle-aged man he did not question, or old man he did not question, or youth

1. This is because when he cannot alter anything except his action and cannot nullify it, he desires that it should not receive a great reward because the reward for the secret action is many times greater than the reward for the public one. This is because the first indicates complete sincerity. This is regarding that which the Messenger of Allah, may Allah bless him and grant him peace, did not make public as he did the prayer and *zakāt* because then its being secret might result in injury to property or in any case, injury in meaning. It is like that with actions that people imitate. These actions must be public so that people can follow those who do them in doing good and in the prescribed path. Shayṭān does not pay attention to desire for this degree. He remains patient for many years in order to forbid the worshipper some of what he deserves because he has been an enemy since the time of our father Adam. The wonder is that he does not despair as he is based on what is false when he tries to make despair infiltrate us, and we have the truth. Allah commanded us to be patient, steadfast and constant. He promised us an immense reward for it: success and well-being in the Next World. Allah says, *'The steadfast will be paid their wages in full without any reckoning.*" (39:10)

he did not question. He would come to one of the houses of the Anṣār, and there would not be any young man he did not question, or middle-aged man he did not question, or old man he did not question, or youth he did not question, He would even try questioning people in chains. How excellent was his behaviour (*adab*) in his lack of concern for beautiful clothes, food or drink, and everything like that!"

Abū 'Uthmān an-Nahdī said, "While we were in Azerbaijan with 'Utba ibn Farqad, a letter reached us from 'Umar ibn al-Khaṭṭāb, may Allah be pleased with him, which said, 'Think little of danger, put on your armour, mount up and set out lightly! Do not wear trousers – you must wear the clothes of your father Ismā'īl, peace be upon him. Beware of appointing the garments of foreigners. You must go into the sun. It is the dear friend of the Arabs.[1] Take on the character of Ma'dd ibn 'Adnān, lead a rough life, become skillful horsemen, ride great distances, and shoot at targets.'"

Abū 'Uthmān 'Abdu'r-Raḥmān an-Nahdī was one of the great Followers, whose life bridged the *Jāhiliyya* period and Islam, although he did not actually see the Messenger of Allah, may Allah bless him and grant him peace. I have clarified his worth in the sciences of *ḥadīth* since he had great importance. He once said,

1 In his advice, 'Umar combined knowledge, wisdom, medicine, welfare, politics and instruction in the art of war. He advised them to keep the clothes of Ismā'īl since they are ample and healthy. The wind passes through them and part of the body is exposed to the sun to derive the benefit of its heat. It is also in order to preserve the customs of the Arab community. He forbade them to wear foreign dress out of the desire to preserve religious customs which are not incompatible with the *Sharī'a*. It is as if he were looking at us from the unseen since European clothes are now an object of pride among us. In some Eastern governments, much blood has been shed in order to propagate European dress. He forbade luxury because it leads to apathy, idleness and laziness which beget cowardice and fear because a community's luxury is its senility and decadence. He ordered them to shoot at targets so that the community would be warlike and study what is connected to war. When they are summoned to *jihād*, they will be ready and able to defend and fight. They will be strong and fit. He ordered them to string their bows and leap on their horses to keep themselves accustomed to activity and to fight on horseback as they fight on foot.

"I have lived for about 130 years, and there has not been anything I did not know except that I advanced to it and discovered it as it is."

When al-Ḥusayn was killed, may Allah be pleased with him, Abū 'Uthmān moved from Kūfa to Baṣra. He said, "I will not live in a city where the grandson of the Messenger of Allah, may Allah bless him and grant him peace, had been murdered!" He died in 55 AH, but some say 100 AH, in Azerbaijan.

It is reported that that Jābir ibn 'Abdullāh al-Anṣārī came to a man to ask about veiling the faults of a believer. He replied, "I do not have any information about that. A man called Shihāb has it." Jābir went to the governor of the town, who was a man called Maslama. He went up to the door and said to the doorman, "Tell the Amīr to come down to me!" The doorman went inside smiling. The Amīr asked him, "What is it?" He replied, "There's a man on a camel who said, 'Tell the Amīr to come down to me!'" The Amīr demanded, "Didn't you ask who it was?" So the doorman went back out and asked him and Jābir replied, "I am Jābir ibn 'Abdullāh al-Anṣārī." The doorman returned to the Amīr and told him. He leapt up from his seat and went to see him. Hetold him, "Come up!" Jābir replied, "I do not want to come up. Tell me where Shihāb lives." He said, "Come up! I will send a messenger to him to get what you want." Jābir said, "I do not want your messenger to go to him. When the messenger of an amīr comes to a man, it alarms him. I don't want to alarm any Muslim on my account."[1] The Amīr came down and walked along with Jābir until they reached Shihāb's house. Shihāb saw them and said, "Will you come up, or shall I come down to you?" Jābir said, "I do not want you to come down to us, and we do not want to go up to you, but tell us a *ḥadīth* you heard from the Messenger of Allah, may Allah bless him and grant him peace, who said, 'Whoever veils his brother, the believer, it is as he had given him life.'"

1. It is because of this love, compassion, *adab* and tenderness to each other that Islam spread out in all lands and the Muslims overcame most of the lands of the world. The unsoundness of this community will only be put right by what put it right in the first place: the behaviour and practice of the noble Companions and virtuous *Salaf.*

Sulaymān ibn Aḥmad ibn Ayyūb aṭ-Ṭabarānī heard Abū Yaḥyā Zakariyyā ibn Yaḥyā as-Sājī say, "One day we were walking in a narrow street in Baṣra on our way to the house of one of the people of *ḥadīth*. I was walking quite rapidly. There was a man with some people who mocked the *dīn* who was making fun of it. He said, 'Take your feet off the angels' wings! Don't break them!' in a very sarcastic fashion. He became rooted to the spot until his feet withered and fell off." 'Abdu'l-Ḥafīẓ said, "This story is based on something like the experience of actually seeing it with one's own eyes, because its transmission was through such distinguished Imāms."

Abū Dāwūd as-Sijistānī was heard to say, "Among the people of *ḥadīth*, there was once a man completely lacking in restraint. He heard the *ḥadīth* of the Prophet, may Allah bless him and grant him peace, which reports that the angels spread out their wings for the seeker of knowledge. He was very pleased with what he was about to do. He put iron nails on his heels and said, 'I want to walk on angels' wings!' He got gangrene in his feet."

Abū 'Abdullāh Muḥammad at-Taymī mentioned this story in his book, *Commentary on the Ṣaḥīḥ Collection of Muslim*. In that version, the man's feet, hands, and all his limbs were paralysed. At-Taymī said, "I also read in another story that one of the innovators heard the words of the Prophet, may Allah bless him and grant him peace, 'When any of you wakes up from sleep, he should not plunge his hand into the water vessel until he has washed it first, since he does not know where his hand has spent the night.' When that innovator heard this, he said derisively, 'I know where my hand has spent the night – in bed!' The next morning, he found that his hand was in his anus up to the forearm." At-Taymī said, "If anyone makes light of the *Sunna* and the limits one should beware of, then he must accept the consequences of his actions!"

The meaning of this *ḥadīth* is explained by what ash-Shāfi'ī and other scholars have said – that when someone is asleep, his hand moves around over his body. He cannot be sure that it has not been in contact with some impurity, like the blood of a flea, a louse or a pustule, or that it has not been in the place of excretion. Allah knows best.

There are many similar incidents which we find in our own time. It has been verified that there was once a man in the village of Busrā at the beginning of 665 AH. He held a very bad opinion about the people of good, but had a son who believed in them. One day his son came home to his father after having been with a shaykh of right action. He had a *siwāk*-stick with him. His father said in a mocking tone of voice, "What's that your shaykh has given you?" His son answered, "This *siwāk*-stick." Then his father took it from him and put it up his anus to show his contempt for it. Some time passed, and then that man execreted something which looked very much like a fish. He killed it, and then he himself died immediately afterwards, or about two days later. May Allah the Generous safeguard us from His punishment! May Allah give us success in exalting the *Sunna* and respecting His signs.

It is reported that Ma'rūf al-Karkhī said, "The sign that Allah hates a servant of His is that you see him occupied with what does not concern him."[1]

Our shaykh, Abū'l-Baqā', related to us that al-Fuḍayl ibn 'Iyāḍ, said, "You ask Him for the Garden while you do what He dislikes! I have never seen anyone with less insight into himself than you!"[2]

Abū'l-Baqā' related to us that Sahl ibn 'Abdullāh said, "There is no veil between the slave and Allah thicker than pretension. There is no quicker way to Him than poverty."[3]

---

1. That is because he opposes the words of the Prophet when he warned against being occupied with what does not concern one. "Part of the excellence of a man's Islam is to leave what does not concern him." Being occupied with what does not concern him does not bring him any good in this world.

2. Since you do two incompatible things. That indicates that your intellect is lacking. If not, you are mocking the commands of Allah. This is a great affliction and the calamity of the greatest punishment. Whoever wants Allah to accept his supplication should offer that which intercede for him: that is fearful awareness of Allah and obeying His commands.

3. Because the first originates in egotism, and so he imitates Iblīs in his claim and his egotism when he said, "I am better than him." The second is the sign of slavenhood. It is the model of the Prophets. They are the best ones to imitate.

Several sound chains of transmission come from Abū Yaḥyā an-Nakrawī on that subject. He said, "I have never seen anyone who was more of a slave to Allah than Shu'ba. His slaveness went to such an extent that his skin dried up on his bones and there was no flesh on them."

We heard that ash-Shāfi'ī said,"The good of this world and the Next World lies in five qualities: the independence of the self, restraint from harm, gaining what is lawful, the safeguard of fear of Allah, and reliance on Allah Almighty in every state."

Ash-Shāfi'ī also said, "Whoever is overcome by intense appetite for this world must venerate and serve its people. Whoever is content with begging has humility removed from him."[1]

Ash-Shāfi'ī stated, "Whoever wants Allah to open his heart and provide him with knowledge must have seclusion, little food and not mix with either fools or those of the people of knowledge who have neither justice nor correct behaviour (*adab*)."

Ash-Shāfi'ī remarked, "The best treasury is safeguarding with fearful awareness, and the worst is enmity."

According to ash-Shāfi'ī "The best actions are three in number: remembrance (*dhikr*) and invocation of Allah, giving out *ṣadaqa* to brothers, and giving justice to people."

"Follow their guidance." He praised the Prophet with slaveness in the noblest station, *"Glory be to Him who took His slave on a journey by night from the Masjid al-Ḥaram to the Masjid al-Aqṣā."* (17:1) One of the qualities of poverty is that the one who has it is related to his Lord. He is "one of My slaves."

1. Contentment/begging. The one who asks has little modesty, so his humility to Allah departs since he is distracted from Him by the people from whom he is seeking his needs. Humility might not even occur to him. Then he moves from slavehood to Allah which is freedom and nobility, to enslavement to mankind. He becomes their slave – abased, insignificant. This is like the two lines ascribed to ash-Shāfi'ī:

The slave is free if he is content,
and the freeman is a slave if he begs.
So be content and do not beg.
Nothing mars except greed.
Al-'abdu ḥurru in qana'
wa'l-ḥurru 'abdun in qana'.
faqna' wa lā taqna' famā
shay'un yashīnu siwā'l-tamā'.

Ash-Shāfi'ī said, "Only someone who is sincere recognises what showing-off is." This means that no one is clearly able to recognise the reality of showing-off and the knowledge of its hidden aspects except someone who desires sincerity. He exerts himself time after time investigating, reflecting and examining until he recognises it or at least recognises some of it. Not every one can obtain it. The elite are the ones who obtain it. As for individuals who claim to recognise showing-off, this is only ignorance on their part.

A great deal is said about the severity of hidden showing-off in the *Risāla* of Abū'l-Qāsim al-Qushayrī. He related that Abū Yazīd al-Bisṭāmī said, "For twelve years I worked as a blacksmith on my *nafs*. For five years, I was the mirror of my heart. For a year I looked upon what stood between them. I saw that I had the belt of an unbeliever clearly around my waist. For twelve years I laboured to sever it Then I looked and there was an unbeliever's belt around my inward part. For five years I laboured to sever it, and thought about how to cut it. Then it was unveiled to me. I looked at mankind and saw them as dead people, and so I said the funeral *takbīrs* over them four times."

This should be enough about the severity of hidden showing-off. It was very obscure even to this master whose like is very rare in this path. He said, "I saw them as dead people." It is at the very limit of excellence. It is rare that one finds it anywhere else except in the words of the Prophet, may Allah bless him and grant him peace. He means by this that when he struggled to the utmost, disciplined his self (*nafs*), had his heart illuminated, overcame his *nafs*, conquered it and ruled over it completely, and it had become completely obedient, then he looked at all creatures and found them as dead, without any power. They could neither harm him nor benefit him, give or withhold, give life or cause to die, connect or sever, come near or go far, make happy or make wretched, provide or deprive, possess any benefit or harm for themselves, or possess either life, or death, or resurrection. This is the attribute of the dead.

He treats them the same way he treats the dead in all these matters. You neither fear anything from them nor hope for anything from them. He does not desire what they have. One does not show off to them or flatter them. He is not occupied with them at all. They are not to be belittled or slighted. You do not mention their faults nor pursue their errors. You do not delve into their mistakes. They are not to be envied, and you do not make a big thing of the blessings which Allah has given them. They are shown mercy and pardoned for whatever imperfections they had, even though we must carry out the *ḥadd*-punishments on them which the *Sharī'a* has stipulated. But making sure the *ḥadd*-punishments are carried out does not prevent us from doing what we have just mentioned. We desire to veil their weaknesses without disparaging them for these weaknesses. That is how you behave with the dead. Whenever someone mentions the dead in a disgraceful manner, we stop him from doing it. We do not do anything to them, and we do not let other people do that to them. We are not prevented from carrying out any acts of obedience to Allah because of them, and we are not prevented from doing that by the dead either. We do not praise them excessively.

We are not affected by their cursing us, neither liking it nor disliking it, and we do not counter it. Finally, it is as if they did not even exist in everything that we have mentioned. They are subject to Allah's management. The judgements of Allah affect them. Whoever treats them in this way has amassed the good of this world and the Next World. We ask Allah, the Generous, for success in this. These few words should be enough as commentary on what he said, but Allah knows best.

Al-Qushayrī related from Shaykh Abū 'Abdu'r-Raḥman as-Sulamī, the Imām of the Sufis in his time and after it, from al-'Abbas al-Baghdādī from Ja'far that al-Junayd heard as-Sarī as-Saqaṭī say, "O company of youths! Strive before you reach my level. You will be weak and incapable just as I was incapable!" In that time, the young men did not keep to performing acts of worship.

Aḥmad ibn Abī'l-Ḥawārī remarked in *The Book of Zuhd* that Suwayd reported that he saw Abū Marthad in the marketplace. He had a bone with meat on it and a loaf of bread in his hand. He was eating this at the same time he was trying to relieve himself. He continued doing that until he was finished.

This is similar to what al-Bayhaqī related from Imām ash-Shāfi'ī. He said, "Sufyān ath-Thawrī came to the Amīr al-Mu'minin. He started to pretend to be mad, and started wiping the carpet. He said, 'I'm doing you a favour – take this!' He cried, 'Urine! Urine!' until he was thrown out. He had tricked them in order to be assured of distance from them and to be safe from their affairs."

Ash-Shāfi'ī said, "A son of al-Ḥusayn ibn 'Alī died but he did not display any sorrow over his loss. He was criticised for that. He answered, 'I am of the people of the House. We ask Allah, and He gives to us. If He wills what we dislike in what He likes, then we are content."

Aḥmad ibn Abī'l-Ḥawārī stated that he heard Abū Sulaymān (ad-Dārānī) say, "We only love those we love because of their obedience to the One who gives them courteous behaviour (*adab*), and yet you rebel against me. I have ordered you to empty your hands."

Sa'īd ibn Jubayr looked at his son and remarked, "Something is lacking in you." His son asked, "What is it?" He replied, "That you die, and that that will be reckoned."

Abū'l-Ḥasan al-Madā'inī reported that it was said to a Bedouin woman, "How excellent is your patience in the loss of your son!" She replied, "The loss of his father made me forget all misfortunes after that."

In order to comfort him over the loss of his son, Mūsā ibn al-Muhtadī told Ibrāhīm ibn Salām, "Your family is a test and a trial. Your sorrow is mercy and prayers." Another man once wrote to one of his brothers to console him over the loss of his son, "If the son lives, he is only a sorrow and a test for his parent. If he goes before him, it is a prayer and a mercy. So do not grieve about the sorrow and the test you have missed. And do not squander and waste what Allah has given you in its place in the way of prayer and mercy!"

Aḥmad ibn al-Ḥawārī said, "I heard Abū Sulaymān say, 'For twenty years I lived without having a wet dream. Then I did something wrong in Makka, and woke up in the morning after having had one.' I asked, 'What did you do?' He replied, 'I did not do the *'Ishā'* prayer in congregation in the Sacred Mosque (*Masjid al-Ḥaram*).'"

Imām Mālik, may Allah be pleased with him, said, "A man can learn and not have a single letter incorrect, and yet all of his actions are incorrect." Abū Bakr Muḥammad ibn Ṣawl al-Mawṣūlī reported that one of the ascetics said, "We speak proper Arabic in our speech and we do not use incorrect Arabic. But we speak incorrectly in our action, so we are not correct!" On this subject, a poet said:

We did not come from ignorance
 but it is with ignorance
that we veil the face of knowledge.

We do not like to use incorrect Arabic in our speech,
 but we do not care
about incorrectness in our actions.

Our Shaykh, Abū Muḥammad ibn Abī'l-Bashīr Shākir related to us that 'Alī ibn Naṣr saw al-Khalīl ibn Aḥmad in a dream. He said to himself, "I have never seen anyone with more intellect than al-Khalīl." So he asked him, "What has Allah done with you?" Khalīl replied, "I saw what we used to do, and there was nothing better than 'Glory be to Allah. Praise be to Allah. There is no god but Allah, and Allah is Greater.'"

In another variant, 'Alī ibn Naṣr said to Khalīl in the dream, "What has your Lord done with you?" to which Khalil replied, "He has forgiven me." He then asked, "And what rescued you?" Khalil answered, "There is no power and no strength except with Allah, the High, the Immense in Splendour." Then 'Alī ibn Naṣr asked him, "And how did you find your knowledge," meaning prosody, literature and poetry. Khalīl replied, "I found it to be nothing more than dust scattered to the four winds."

It is reported from Abū Bakr an-Najjār that Hilāl ibn al-'Alā' composed these lines for himself.

A tongue speaking excellent Arabic
will be put to the test –
Would that it were safe
in the place of Presentation!

The Arabs will not be helped
if they have no fearful awareness
and even unintelligible speech will not harm
those who possess fear of Allah!

Chapter 6

The Miracles and Gifts of the *Awliyā'*

Allah Almighty says:

> *"Yes, the friends of Allah will feel no fear and will know no sorrow: those who believe and are godfearing, there is good news for them in the life of this world and in the Next World. There is no changing the words of Allah. That is the great victory!"* (10:63-65)

Know that the school of the people of Allah is to affirm the miracles of the friends of Allah (*awliyā'*) and to acknowledge the fact that they occur and exist in all ages. This is indicated by logical proofs and explicit transmissions. The logical proof is that it is within the realm of possibility that they could occur and still their occurence would in no way lead to the removal or contravention of any of the roots of the *dīn*. To Allah we must attribute the power to perform miracles. Whatever He has the power to perform can conceivably happen. This is the logical proof.

The explicit transmissions are *āyats* in the Immense Qur'an and the detailed traditions of the Prophet, may the peace and blessings of Allah be upon him. One of these *āyats* are the words of Allah about the mercy shown to Maryam:

> *"Shake the trunk of the palm towards you and fresh, ripe dates will drop down onto you."* (19:25)

Al-Juwaynī said that Maryam was not a Prophet. There is a consensus among scholars about this. Others have said the same thing, and they also say that she was a truthful friend (*walīya*) just as Allah reports regarding her, saying:

"Every time Zakariyyā visited her in the Upper Room, he found food with her. He said, 'Maryam, how did you come by this?' She said, 'It is from Allah. Allah provides for whoever He wills without any reckoning.'" (3:37)

Another instance is the story of the companion of the Prophet Sulaymān, peace be upon him, who said, *"I will bring it you before your glance returns to you."* (27:40) Scholars say that this companion was not a Prophet.

Another example is the story of the mother of the Prophet Mūsā which al-Juwaynī and others used as a proof.

Yet another example is the story of Dhū'l-Qarnayn which al-Qushayrī used as a proof.

Another example is the story of al-Khiḍr in his encounter with Mūsā, peace be upon him, which al-Qushayrī and others used as a evidence. They said that he was not a Prophet. He was a friend (*walī*). But this is at variance with the preferred opinion of most people that al-Khiḍr was a Prophet. Some say that he was a Prophet-Messenger while others say that he was a *walī*. Others say that he was an angel. I have explained and clarified this disagreement in my books, *The Instruction of the Names and Languages* and *The Commentary of the Disciplined.*[1] Another example is the

1. They disagree about the life al-Khiḍr and his Prophethood. Most scholars say that he is alive and among us now. The Sufis and the righteous agree about that. Their stories about seeing him, meeting him, learning from him, questioning him, and his answer, and his presence are too numerous and well-known to mention. Abū 'Amr ibn aṣ-Ṣalāḥ said in his *Opinions* that he is alive according to most of the scholars, righteous and common people. He said that it is very rare that it be rejected by one of the people of *ḥadith.* He said that he is a Prophet. They disagree about his being a Messenger. Other people have said the same as this shaykh said.

Abū'l-Qāsim al-Qushayrī said in his *Risāla* in the Chapter of *Awliyā'* that al-Khiḍr was not a Prophet. He says that he was a *walī*. Al-Māwardī said in his *Commentary* that it is said that he is a *walī,* it is said that he is a Prophet and it is said that he is one of the angels. This third opinion is very unusual and weak or false. At the end of the *Ṣaḥīḥ* collection of Muslim it is said in the *ḥadīth* about the Dajjāl that he will kill a man and then bring him to life. Ibrāhīm ibn Sufyan, Muslim's companion, said that it is said that that man is al-Khiḍr. Ma'mar also stated in his *Musnad* that it is al-Khiḍr. Abū Isḥāq ath-Tha'labī, the commentator,

story of the people of the Cave, and the miracle that breaks normal patterns that takes place in it. The consensus of al-Juwaynī and others is that the people of the Cave were not Prophets.

The *ḥadīths* on this subject are very numerous. One of them is the *ḥadīth* transmitted by Anas, that when two of the Companions left the Prophet's presence, may Allah bless him and grant him peace, one dark night, there was something like two lamps giving off light in front of them, and when they parted company, a lamp went ahead of each of them until they reached their families. Al-Bukhārī reports it in his *Ṣaḥīḥ* collection in the *Book of Prayer* and *The Signs of Prophethood.* The names of of these two men were 'Abbād ibn al-Bishr and Usayd ibn Ḥuḍayr.

Another *ḥadīth* concerning friends of Allah is about the three companions who took shelter in a cave, and a stone rolled in front of the opening, trapping them inside. Each of them made a supplication to Allah, and finally the stone rolled away for them. This tradition appears in the *Ṣaḥīḥ* collections of Muslim and al-Bukhārī.

Abū Hurayra reports the story of Jurayḥ (a hermit). He asked a baby, "Who is your father?" and the child replied, "Such-and-such, the shepherd." This *ḥadīth* is found in the *Ṣaḥīḥ* collections.

In another *ḥadīth,* also reported by Abu Hurayra, the Prophet, may Allah bless him and grant him peace, said, "There were inspired people in the communities before you. If there is another one in my community, it is 'Umar." Another variant reads, "In those before you among the tribe of Isrā'īl, there were people who were inspired to speak without being Prophets." Al-Bukhārī related it in his *Ṣaḥīḥ* Collection.

The story of Khubayb al-Anṣārī, the Companion of the Prophet, may Allah bless him and grant him peace appears in the *Ṣaḥīḥ* Collection of al-Bukhārī as well as other sources. The daughter of al-Ḥārith said about him, "By Allah, I have never seen a better

---

mentioned a disagreement about al-Khiḍr and whether he lived in the time of Ibrāhīm the Friend or a little after him. He said that everyone affirms that al-Khiḍr is a living Prophet, who is veiled from the eyes. He also stated that it is said that he will not die until the end of time when the Qur'ān is removed.

prisoner than Khubayb. By Allah, one day I found him eating a bunch of grapes from his hand while he was wearing iron shackles, and there was no fruit at all in Makka." She added. "It was by Allah's provision with which He provided Khubayb."

The *ḥadīths*, traditions and statements of the *Salaf* and the later ones are too numerous to even begin to enumerate. What has been mentioned should suffice.

Al-Juwaynī stated that the breaking of normal patterns, what are commonly called miracles, in respect to the friends of Allah (*awliyā'*) is perfectly conceivable. The Mu'tazilites reject that. Some of the people of Allah stipulated as a precondition for the miracle that breaks normal patterns that it be without personal preference of choice on the part of the *walī* himself. These people say that this is what distinguishes the miracle that breaks patterns from the prophetic miracle. The Imām says, "This statement is not valid." Others allow that the breaking of norms can occur within the principle of choice, but they say that it cannot happen simply to support a claim. They said, "When the *walī* lays claim to *wilāya*, and seeks to support his claim through the confirmation of a miracle, that is forbidden." By this definition, they differentiate between ordinary miracles and prophetic miracles.

The Imām said, "This definition does not suffice either. In our opinion, it is not impossible for miracle to appear when there is an assumed claim. One of our companions went so far as to say that whatever miracles took place for a Prophet are not permitted to be miracles of a *walī*. Therefore he thinks that it is impossible for any *walī* to part the sea, turn a staff into a snake, bring the dead to life, or anything similar among the signs of the Prophets. But this sort of definition is not correct. What we find acceptable, on the contrary, is that it is possible for normal patterns to be broken in order to display miracles (*karāmāt* = lit. marks of honour). Our goal in invalidating these schools and methods is to affirm what we consider to be sound. As for the distinction between them as far as the intellect is concerned, other than the fact that the prophetic miracle occurs in accordance with the claim to prophethood, while the other miracle occurs without the claim to prophethood."

He goes on to state, "There were signs that occurred at the birth of the Messenger of Allah, may Allah bless him and grant him peace, which no one who belongs to Islam rejects. These signs took place before he was given Prophethood, and before he was sent as a Messenger. The Prophetic miracle does not precede the claim to Prophethood. It is simply a miracle (*karāma*). If someone arbitrarily claims that the signs which we use as proofs are Prophetic miracles which belong to a Prophet in every age, then he is simply rushing in out of his own ignorance. If we investigate the past ages, we will not find the signs we are holding onto as connected to a claim of Prophethood, nor do they occur simply as a result of a provocation by a challenger. If they say that they only occur for the Prophets rather than for the common people, we say that a claim is a precondition for a Prophetic miracle. If that claim is lacking, then the breaking of normal patterns is a *"karāma"* of the Prophets. That is the point we want to make in affirming miracles. At the time of the birth of our Prophet Muḥammad, may Allah bless him and grant him peace, he was not a Prophet with a claim supported by signs."

The Imām goes on further to say, "I have made it clear that miracles are possible, and do occur, both by intellectual proofs and by what is contained in tradition." The Imām, as well as others, distinguishes between a miracle and sorcery. Only someone who has strayed from the right way manifests sorcery. He said that this conclusion is not based on intellectual demands, but it is reported from the consensus of the community. He said that a miracle is not manifested by a person who has deviated from the right way and makes his deviation public. This can never bear witness to his *wilāya*. If it had borne witness to that, people would have been safe from the results. That is absolutely not permissible for a *walī* in a miracle. Everyone agrees on this. This is the last of what al-Juwaynī said.

Abū'l-Qāsim al-Qushayrī stated in his *Risāla*, "The manifestation of miracles is a token of the truthfulness of the states of the one who manifests them. It is not impossible for someone who is not truthful to manifest any miracles like these. The miracle must be an action that breaks the normal pattern of things during the ordinary days of religious obligation. It appears connected to the one who is described as a *walī*, in order to confirm his truthfulness about his state." He goes to discuss the difference between the Prophetic miracle and the miracle (*karāma*).

He quotes Abū Isḥāq al-Isfrāyinī who said, "Prophetic miracles are the proofs of the truthfulness of the Prophets. The proof of Prophethood does not exist with someone who is not a Prophet."

He used to say, "The *awliyā'* have miracles which resemble having supplications answered. But as for the *awliyā'* having miracles associated with the Messengers of Allah, I say no to this."

Abū Bakr ibn Furāk said, "Prophetic miracles are proofs of truthfulness. If the one who possesses them claims to be a Prophet, then they are a proof of his truthfulness. If the one who has them claims to be a *walī*, then they are a proof of his truthfulness in that state. Then it is called a *karāma* and not a Prophetic miracle. It is not even called a Prophetic miracle if it is the same as a Prophetic miracle, because of the distinction between them."

Abū Bakr ibn Furāk goes on to say, "Part of the difference between Prophetic miracles and *karāmāt* is that the Prophets, blessings and peace of Allah be upon all of them, are commanded to display their miracles while the *walī* is obliged to veil and conceal them. The Prophet makes a claim, and his statement is substantiated by the confirmatory miracle. The *walī* does not make that claim, and it is not substantiated by the miracle since it is equally possible that the occasion for claim could occur through deception."

Qāḍī Abū Bakr al-Ash'arī said, "Prophetic miracles were the priviledge of the Prophets. *Karāmāt* are manifested for both the *awliyā'* and the Prophets. Then *awliyā'* do not have Prophetic miracles because one of the preconditions of the Prophetic miracle is that it should be connected to the claim of Prophethood. The Prophetic miracle is not in itself a Prophetic miracle. It becomes a Prophetic miracle when it possesses several qualities. When any one of these preconditions is lacking, then it is not a Prophetic miracle. One of these preconditions is the claim to Prophethood. The *walī* does not claim to be a Prophet, so what he manifests is not a Prophetic miracle."

Al-Qushayrī said, "What he states is what we support and accept. All the preconditions – or at least most of them – of the Prophetic miracle exist in *karāmāt* except for this one condition. A *karāma* is an action about which there is no doubt. It breaks the normal patterns, and the slave of Allah obtains it during the time he is responsible for the obligatory duties of his *dīn*. It is a gift and a mark of favour on him. It may be obtained by the choosing and supplication of the *walī*, while it is also possible that it will not be obtained by him. Sometimes it is without any choice on the part of the *walī*. The *walī* is not commanded to call people to himself. Even if he manifests anything of what would make him worthy of it, that is still not permissible.

"The people of Allah disagree about the *walī* as to whether or not it is permissible for him to know that he is a *walī*. Abū Bakr ibn Fūrāk said, 'It is not possible, because it would strip fear away from him, and he would then be secure in what he has.'

"Abū 'Alī ad-Daqqāq said that it is permissible. That is the view we prefer, and the one we affirm. But it is not obligatory for each and every one of the *awliyā'* to know that he is a *walī*. It is, however, conceivable that some of them know it while others of them do not. If one of the *awliyā'* knows he is a *walī*, his recognition of it is one of his miracles which he alone has.

"Not every miracle of a *walī* must necessarily be possessed by all of the *awliyā'*. Indeed, if a *walī* does not have outwardly manifest *karāmāt* in this world, their lack does not detract from his being a *walī*, unlike the Prophets.[1] The Prophets must have Prophetic miracles since a Prophet is someone sent to creation, and the people must recognise his truthfulness, and that is only confirmed by the Prophetic miracle. But the state of the *walī* is the

1. It seems that he means the Prophets who are sent with a *Sharī'a* because those are the ones from whom people require a miracle to prove their truthfulness to follow their *Sharī'a*. A Prophet is a man to whom a *Sharī'a* is revealed. If he is not commanded to convey it, he remains not commanded to convey it. Therefore, he does not need a miracle.

reverse of that, and this is because neither the creation nor the *walī* himself are obliged to know that he is a *walī.*

"Ten of the Companions, may Allah be pleased with them, were confirmed by the Messenger of Allah, may Allah bless him and grant him peace, as being the people of Paradise. If someone says that this is not permissible since it removes all fear from them, we assert that there is no harm at all in not fearing any change in their end. What is in their hearts of awe, exaltation and glorification of Allah increases even more than fear."

Then al-Qushayri said, "The *walī* must not rely on any miracle that has manifested itself through him. He should not pay any attention to it. Whenever they manifest miracles, they have a certain power and increased inner vision, because they realise that it was, in fact, the act of Allah, and not from themselves. They take the manifestation of miracles as proof of the validity of their creed." But Allah knows best.

Section 1

Al-Qushayrī, may Allah have mercy on him, said, "If it is said, 'How can *karāmāt* be manifested which intensify the meanings of the miracles of the Messenger?' we reply that this *karāma* is closely related to the Prophetic miracles of our Prophet Muḥammad, may Allah bless him and grant him peace, because of the fact that whoever is not truthful in Islam is kept from miracles. Whenever a Prophet has a miracle appear through one of his community, that miracle is also counted as one of his Prophetic miracles. If the Messenger had not been truthful, then the Prophetic miracle would not have appeared through anyone who followed him."

*****

Al-Qushayrī said, "Can a *walī* be preferred over the Prophet? We say that the rank of the *awliyā'* does not reach the rank of the Prophets, blessings and peace of Allah be upon all of them. There is a general consensus on this."

*****

Al-Qushayri said, "These miracles are an answer to supplication. They may manifest as food in times of poverty, apppearing without any apparent cause. They may consist of obtaining water in a time of drought, or easily crossing a distance in a very short time, or being relieved of an enemy, or hearing words spoken by an invisible voice, or any of these kinds of extraordinary occurences."

He said, "It is well-known today that there are many abilities it is are absolutely not permissible for the *awliyā'* to display either by necessity or anything approaching necessity. One of these is that a man should come into existence without two parents, that a stone should turn into a beast, or anything like that."

Al-Qushayrī said, "As for the meaning of *walī, it* may be one of two things. It may come from the intensive active form of the noun (*fa'īl*), like the knower (*'alīm*) or the the one with power (*qadīr*), and so it means that his obedience continues unbroken by any act of rebellion. The second possibility for *walī* is that the form of the noun has a passive sense, like "corpse (*qatīl*)", which means someone who has been slain, or "injured (*jarīḥ*)". This is the *walī* whom Allah undertakes to constantly guard and preserve Himself. He manages him, so that this *walī* never has the disappointment which is possible in an act of rebellion. His success is enduring, since it is part of the constant capacity of obedience. Allah says: *"He takes care of the righteous."* (7:196)

*****

As for someone who does actions that are righteous, that refers to the Prophet as well as the *walī*. Allah says:

> *"And Ismā'īl and Idrīs and Dhū'l-Kifl – each one was among the steadfast. We admitted them into Our mercy. They were among the righteous."* (21:85-86)

Allah says:

> *'They will be with those whom Allah has blessed: the Prophets, the men of truth, the martyrs, and the righteous."* (4:69)

One sound *ḥadīth* states that the Prophet, may Allah bless him and grant him peace, stated about 'Abdullah ibn 'Umar, "He is a righteous man." There are many *ayats* of Qur'ān and *ḥadīths* along these lines which I have not included here.

As for the definition of 'righteous' or *ṣāliḥ*, Abū Isḥāq az-Zajjāj said in his book, *The Meanings of the Qur'ān* as did Abū Isḥāq ibn Qarqūl, the author of *The Ascents of Lights*: "He is someone who fulfils his obligations in regard to the rights of Allah and the rights of His slaves."

✲✲✲✲✲

Imam al-Qushayrī said, "If it is asked if the *walī* is protected from wrong action or not, the answer is that if it is the same sense as the Prophets are protected, they are not. As for the *walī* being protected so that he does not persist in wrong actions, even if sometimes he commits errors or slips, that is not impossible for them. This question was asked of al-Junayd, who replied, "The gnostic commits adultery, travels a long distance, then lifts his head and says, *'Allah's command is a pre-ordained decree.'* (33:38)"

✲✲✲✲✲

Al-Qushayrī said, "If it is asked if fear falls away from the *awliyā'*, we state that all the great *awliyā'* are dominated by fear. It is rare for fear to fall away, but not impossible. As-Sarī as-Saqaṭī said, 'If anyone were to enter a garden with many trees in it, and there was a bird on each tree saying in the most eloquent voice, "Peace be upon you, *walī* of Allah," and he had no fear that it might be a deception, he would certainly be deceived by it.' There are numerous examples of this in their stories.

If it is asked if it may be possible for a *walī* to be free of the fear of deceit, we say that if he is absorbed in what he witnesses and swept away from the sensation of his state, then he is free of it while he is overwhelmed. Fear is one of the attributes of those who are fully present."

✲✲✲✲✲

Al-Qushayrī said, "If it were to be asked what dominates a *walī* in the state of sobriety, we would say that it is his truthfuless in fulfilling the duties owed to Allah Almighty. Then it is his compassion and mercy to the people of creation in all their states. Then it is extending his mercy to all creatures. Then it is constantly enduring things that come from creatures with good character. He always begins by asking Allah to do the best for them without their having to ask this of him. His zeal (*himma*) is connected to rescuing the people and giving them security. He safeguards himself from feeling any malice or rancour towards them, while at the same time he restrains his hand from their property and desires nothing from them in any way. He restrains his tongue from spreading any evil about them, and he is on guard against seeing their evils. He has no adversary either in this world or in the Next World."[1]

He means by this that the *walī* overlooks his own rights in this world, so that he demands nothing from people in this world. Therefore, they possess nothing which he will seek from them in the Next World either. Allah says:

> *"But if you are steadfast and godfearing, that is the most resolute course to take."* (3:186)

Allah says:

> *"Those who control their rage and pardon other people. Allah loves the good-doers."* (3:134)

1. This is truly the attribute of the believer. Its being a special quality of the *walī* might lead people to believe that they are incapable of reaching these actions because they are particular to the *awliyā'* and *wilāya* is a gift from Allah to whomever He likes which man cannot reach by striving. Many Sufis make the business so alarming that most people believe that it is beyond them to attain the rank of *wilāya*. However, *wilāya* is going straight in the *Sharī'a* of Muhammad and following the rules of the *dīn* and the attributes which they have mentioned. Allah commanded that and told people to act according to it, so it is not something difficult or a miracle. It is necessary for every Muslim. Whoever does not do it has gaps in his beliefs – except for the perfect actions which can be done and for which there is no punishment if they are not done. I wish that they would say *"mūmin"* instead of *"walī"* so that the resolution of the Muslim would not falter and he will believe that it is not in his capacity to realise these prescribed beneficial qualities. Most of them are in the *ḥadīths* which have been mentioned in this book. All of them are taken from the Book and the *Sunna*.

In the book, *The Actions of the Day and Night*, by Ibn as-Sunnī, it is reported that Anas ibn Malik mentioned that the Messenger of Allah, may Allah bless him and grant him peace, said, "Is any of you incapable of being like Abū Damdam?" They replied, "Who is Abū Damdam, Messenger of Allah?" He said, "In the morning, he says, 'O Allah! I have given my self and honour to You,' so consequently he does not abuse someone who abuses him, he does not wrong someone who wrongs him and he does not strike anyone who strikes him.'" This means that he does not seek retaliation from anyone who wrongs him, as Allah says:

> *"So if anyone oversteps the limits against you, overstep against him the same as he did to you."* (2:194)

*****

Al-Qushayrī said, "Know that it is because of the *karāmāt* the *awliyā'* have that their success in obedience continues, as well as their being protected from any acts of rebellion."

Acts of opposition are rare for them. Any action which is not rebellious may be included under actions of opposition, like an action which is disapproved of, such as not refraining from an appetite which has been recommended to us to refrain from."

*****

Al-Qushayrī said, "If it is asked if it is possible to see the Creator with one's eyes at this moment in this world as a *karāma,* we say that the strongest position is that it is not possible since there is consensus about that. I heard Abū Bakr ibn Furāk, may Allah be pleased with him, relate that Abū'l-Ḥasan al-Ash'arī said that there are two positions regarding that. He mentioned this in *The Book of the Great Vision"*

The consensus of opinion is that the *awliyā'* do not receive the vision of Allah in this world. That is not due to its impossibility. It is intellectually possible according to the People of Allah. The Companions themselves, and those after them, disagreed about whether or not the Prophet, may Allah bless him and grant him peace, saw his Lord on the Night Journey. The best view among most people is that he saw Him. That is the statement of Ibn 'Abbās. I have dealt with this in the *Commentary on the Ṣaḥīḥ of Muslim.*

*****

Al-Qushayrī said, "If it is asked if it is possible for someone to be a *walī* and then have his end change, we said that someone who makes the excellent fulfilment of the *dīn* a precondition for *wilāya* does not allow for that. Someone else may say that, in reality, he is a believer in that state. If it is possible for his state to change, then it is not inconceivable that he be a *walī,* truthful in that state, and then change. This is the view we prefer. It is also conceivable that one of the miracles of the *walī* be that he know that his end is secure and that it will not change. This question is closely related to what has already been mentioned about the *walī* being able to know that he is a *walī.*"

Section 2
Various Stories about Gifts and Miracles

We have already clarified the definition of miracles. Gifts are something which do not involve the breaking of normal patterns. Nevertheless, the gift is a rare and unusual occurrence as far as the normal pattern is concerned. Only some people are singled out for it, and it is not exclusive to the *awliyā'*. Gifts are possible both to the *awliyā'* and to other people. In this chapter will be mentioned some miracles and excellent gifts, if Allah wills. Allah says:

> *"We have given you all this news about the Messengers so We can make your heart firm by means of it."* (11:120)

He also says:

> *'They are the ones Allah has guided, so be guided by their guidance."* (6:90)

Our Shaykh, Abū Muḥammad 'Abdu'r-Raḥmān ibn Qudāma, reported from Abū Sa'īd al-Khudrī that the Messenger of Allah, may Allah bless him and grant him peace, said. "A believer does not fill up with some good that he hears but that he ends up in the Garden." At-Tirmidhī said that it is an excellent *ḥadīth*.

He also reported that 'Umar ibn Hāni' used to pray a thousand *rak'ats* a day and to glorify Allah a hundred thousand times.

Abū Muslim al-Khawlānī

Our Shaykh, Abū'l-Baqā' related to us that 'Aṭā' said, "The wife of Abū Muslim al-Khawlānī said, 'Abū Muslim, we have no flour!' He said, 'Have you got anything?' She replied, 'Only a dirham which we got for my spinning.' He said, 'Then give it to me and give me the bag.' He went to the market and stood in front of a man selling food. Then a beggar came to him and said, 'Abu Muslim! Give me some *ṣadaqa*!' He fled from the beggar and went to another shop, but the beggar followed him, saying, 'Give us some *ṣadaqa*!' Finally, exasperated, he gave him the dirham. Then he took the bag and filled it with woodshavings from the carpenter's and some dirt. He took the bag of his house, but he did not want to go in because his heart was filled with fear of his family. So he opened the door, threw in the sack and left.

"When his wife opened the sack, it contained white flour. She mixed it up, kneaded it and made bread. After the beginning of the night had passed, Abū Muslim came to the house, but he still did not want to go in. When he finally came in, his wife set the table and placed some white loaves on it in front of him. He said, 'Where did you get this?'

"She replied, 'Abū Muslim, it is from the flour you brought!' He began to eat and weep at the same time." How precious a story this is! How full of benefit!

Abū Muslim's name was 'Abdullah ibn Thuwāb. He is also called Ibn Thawāb or Ibn Athwab and is also referred to as Ibn 'Abdullāh or Ibn 'Awf or Ibn Yaslam. It is also said that his name was Ya'qūb ibn 'Awf. However the sound and most well-known version is the one we have mentioned. He was from the people of Yemen, and settled in Dāriya, a village near Damascus. He was one of the great *Tābi'ūn*. He was one of the people who have outward *karāmāt* and radiant apparent states. He set off on a journey to the Messenger of Allah, may Allah bless him and grant him peace, to become his Companion. but the Prophet, may Allah bless him and grant him peace, died while he was on his way to him. He arrived and met Abū Bakr, 'Umar and other Companions.

One of the rare *karāmāt* of Abū Muslim is related by Imam Aḥmad ibn Ḥanbal in *The Book of Zuhd*. In it he says that Abū Muslim al-Khawlānī passed by the Tigris River while it was casting wood up onto the shore. He walked out on top of the water, then turned to his companions and said, "Do you lack any of your necessities? Then call on Allah, the Mighty, the Majestic!"

It is related from another chain of transmission that he stood beside the Tigris. He praised Allah, mentioned His blessings, then spoke of the journey of the Tribe of Israel through the sea. At that, he drove his pack-animal onward and plunged into the Tigris. The people followed him until everyone had passed through the river.

Ibn Ḥanbal also related that Abū Muslim was once in Byzantine territory when the governor had sent out a raiding party and had set a definite time for it to attack. The party had tarried beyond the time and Abū Muslim was worried about their delay. While he was doing *wuḍū'* at the edge of a river and talking to himself about their situation, a crow came and perched on a tree opposite him. It said, "Abū Muslim! You are worried about the raiding-party!"

Abū Muslim replied, "Indeed I am!"

The crow said, "Don't worry. They are busy plundering, and will get to you on such-and-such a day at such-and-such a time."

Abū Muslim said, "Who are you, may Allah have mercy on you?"

It said, "I gladden the hearts of the believers." The raiding-party arrived at the time the crow had mentioned, and on the day it had mentioned."

Ibn Ḥanbal also related that one day Abū Muslim was in Byzantine territory sitting and conversing with his companions. They said, "Abū Muslim, we would like some meat. If you were to call upon Allah, he would provide us with it."

He said, "O Allah! You have heard what they are saying, and You have the power to do what they ask!" Suddenly they heard the shouts of the army. A gazelle rushed forward and passed right in front of Abū Muslim and his companions. They rushed off and seized it.

Ibn Ḥanbal also related that once there was a drought while Mu'āwiya was khalif. Abū Muslim went out with them to do the prayer of petition for rain. When they reached the place for the prayer, Mu'āwiya said to Abū Muslim, "You see the plight of the people. Call on Allah!"

Abū Muslim replied, "I will do that on a certain condition." Then he stood up wearing a burnoose. He took off his burnoose, raised his hands and said, "O Allah, we ask You for rain! I have come to You with my wrong actions, so do not disappoint me." It began raining before they left the place. Then Abū Muslim said, "O Allah, Mu'āwiya put me in a position which will give me reputation with people. If I have something better than that with You, then take me to You!" He said this on a Thursday and he died the following Thursday, may Allah be pleased with him!

Shuraḥbīl ibn Muslim said that when Al-Aswad ibn Qays al-'Anasī the Liar claimed to be a Prophet in the Yemen, he sent for Abū Muslim al-Khawlānī. When Abū Muslim came before him, Al-Aswad said to him, "Do you testify that I am the the Prophet?"

Abū Muslim said, "I cannot hear."

Then al-Aswad the Liar said, "Do you testify that Muḥammad is the Messenger of Allah?"

Abū Muslim replied, "Yes." Then al-Aswad repeated his questioning of him, and after that commanded a great fire to built. When it was kindled, he threw Abū Muslim into it but it did not harm him. Then someone told al-Aswad, "Send Abū Muslim away or he will turn your followers against you." So he ordered him to leave. Abū Muslim journeyed to Madina and arrived after the Messenger of Allah, may Allah bless him and grant him peace, had died. Abū Bakr, may Allah be pleased with him, had become the khalif. Abū Muslim made his camel kneel at the door of the mosque and began to pray in front of one of columns. 'Umar saw him and went to him. He asked him, "Where are you from?"

Abū Muslim replied, "From the people of Yemen."

'Umar said, "Perhaps you are the one whom the Liar burned in the fire?"

Abū Muslim replied, "That was 'Abdullāh ibn Thawāb."

'Umar said, "I ask you by Allah, are you him?"

Abū Muslim answered, "O Allah, yes." Then 'Umar embraced him and wept. He took him with him and sat him down between himself and Abū Bakr. Abū Muslim said, "Praise be to Allah, Who did not let me die before I had found myself in the community of Muḥammad, may Allah bless him and grant him peace." Allah did with him as He did with Ibrāhīm, the Close Friend of the Merciful, peace be upon him.

This is one of the most glorious *karāmāt*, and one of the rarest radiant states. He said, "I can't hear," and it can have two possible meanings. One of them is that he meant by that, "I do not accept that you are the Messenger of Allah." the second is that it means literally that he could not hear, that Allah had stopped up his hearing against this false, deviant claim. Some of the Imams limit the meaning of his statement to the first possibility, but I think that the second meaning is clearer.

*****

Aḥmad Ibn Abi'l-Ḥawārī related in his book, *The Book of Zuhd*, that 'Abdu'l-Waḥid ibn Ziyād was afflicted with semi-paralysis. He asked Allah to give him strength at the times of doing *wuḍū'*. When it was time for him to do *wuḍū'*, he would get up from his bed and perform his *wuḍū'*. Then he would return to his bed and the semi-paralysis would come back to him. Allah knows best.

Al-Qushayrī mentioned that Abū Ḥātim as-Sijistānī said that he heard Abū Naṣr as-Sarrāj say, "We entered Tustar and found that the people called the house which belonged to Sahl ibn 'Abdullāh "The House of Wild Beasts." We asked the people why, and they replied that wild beasts used to come to Sahl, go into his house, and he would treat them as guests, feed them meat, and then send them on their way." Abū Naṣr said, "All of the people of Tustar were in agreement about this, and there were many of them."

Abū'l-Khayr

Al-Qushayrī related that Ḥamza ibn 'Abdullāh al-'Alawī said, "I went to visit Abū'l-Khayr at-Tinatī with the firm resolve that I would just greet him and leave, and that I would not stay to eat any food with him. So I left him and walked on and when I had gone a short distance, he suddenly came up behind me carrying a plate of food. He said, 'Young man, eat this! I have, at this instant, brought you out of your previous conviction.'" Abū'l-Khayr was famous for his miracles.

Ibrāhīm ar-Raqqī said, "I went to visit Abū'l-Khayr. He prayed the *Maghrib* prayer and did not recite the *Fātiḥa* well. I said to myself, 'My journey has been wasted.' After he had pronounced the final salutation, I went outside to do *wuḍū'*. A lion started to attack me, so I went back inside and said to him, 'A lion is after me!' He went out and shouted at the lion, saying, 'Didn't I tell you not to bother my guests?' So the lion went away and I did *wuḍū'*. When I went back in, he said, 'You have been busy putting the outward in order, so you are afraid of the lion. We have been busy putting the heart in order, so the lion is afraid of us!'"

Someone who is like the *fuqahā'* but without real *fiqh* might imagine that the prayer of Abū'l-Khayr was invalid because he did not recite the *Fātiḥa* well, but that would just be ignorance and stupidity. Whenever anyone conceives of suppositions against any of the *awliyā'* of Allah, it is to his own loss. The intelligent man is always on his guard against doing this. If he himself does not understand their fundamentals and their excellent subtle expressions, he should seek someone who does understand and find out from him how to recognise them. If someone without realisation thinks this sort of thing is an offense, know that it is not an offense. The actions of the *awliyā'* of Allah must be interpreted correctly.

In this case there are three possible answers to the fact that Abū'l-Khayr did not recite the *Fātiḥa* well. The first is that there was a fault in the grammar of the Arabic which did not affect the meaning. But it is generally agreed that this does not invalidate the prayer. The second is that he had a speech defect and it is generally agreed that his prayer would be valid if he did. The third view is that even if none of the first two reasons were right, Abū Ḥanīfa and a group of scholars did not specifically impose the recitation of the *Fātiḥa* for the prayer. Therefore this *walī* is not obliged to follow the school that obliges it. I saw this story recounted in the handwriting of the Shaykh himself, may Allah be pleased with him.

Chapter 7

Some Excellent Stories

Ar-Rāzī said, "I attended a gathering of Sulaymān ibn Ḥarb in Baghdad. There were more than 40,000 people present at his assembly, which took place at the palace of al-Ma'mūn. Al-Ma'mūn had ordered a *minbar* built for him and Sulaymān would climb up onto it. Al-Ma'mūn remained in the upper part of his palace, where he had opened up his door and set up a thin curtain. He sat behind the curtain writing down what Sulaymān dictated. Al-Ma'mūn was asked about the first thing Sulaymān related from Hushaym ibn 'Uqayl. He might have stated, 'We related from Hushaym ibn 'Uqayl...' more than ten times. Finally they told him, 'You cannot hear him.' Then the group asked, 'Do you not think that the person taking dictation should be present?' So a group of them went and brought him. When al-Ma'mūn was there, he asked, 'Who did you mention?' and Sulaymān's voice was like thunder. Everyone was silent, and all those taking down dictation sat down, and Hārūn took dictation."

Ar-Rāzī added, "He did not ask about the *ḥadīth* of the later one from the one who had heard him." Abū Sa'īd as-Sam'ānī said that there were 10,000 men present at a session of dictation from Qāḍī Abū 'Abdullāh al-Muḥamilī.

In various places, I saw that the Shaykh, may Allah have mercy on him, wrote that, "I heard our master and imām, Zaynu'd-dīn, may Allah be pleased with him, speak twice. The last time was Wednesday, 3 Ramaḍan 657. He said that Shaykh Shihābu'd-dīn as-Suhrawardī delivered an exhortation in Damascus. Al-A'azz ibn Ja'far recited Qur'an and the Shaykh went into an ecstasy and gave him his garment. One of the men present, Jamālu'd-dīn, bought it for five hundred dirhams because of the blessing *(baraka)* it possessed. He did not let any of his time go to waste. He was always engaged in prayer, recitation and *dhikr*. Our Shaykh, may Allah be pleased with him, wore a *khirqa* which he took from him and he kept his company for some time in Baghdad in the *ribāṭ*."

I heard our Shaykh, Abū Ismā'īl Muḥammad ibn Ibrahim relate that Shaykh Muḥammad al-Bursī, said, "We were visiting the *ḥāfiẓ*, 'Abdu'l-Ghanī, and there was a group of people from a larger group who were asking for *fatwās*. When he placed his foot on the rung of the chair. I said to myself, 'Why has Allah preferred him over us?' He turned to me at once and said, 'O manager of the one who serves the servant of the one who serves the servant of the one who serves the servant!' I said, 'I have believed in Allah.'"

I heard our master, Shaykh Kamālu'd-dīn Silār relate that one of the *fuqahā'* placed the text of *The Disciplined* under his head as a pillow and then went to sleep. He had a wet-dream and saw Shaykh Abū Isḥāq, the author of *The Disciplined* in his dream. He kicked him with his foot and said to him, 'Sit up! Isn't it enough that you put *The Disciplined* under your head and then became impure!'"

I heard our Shaykh and master, the scholar, 'Izzu'd-dīn Abū Ja'far 'Umar As'ad ibn Abī Ghālib al-Aylī, the Shāfi'ī *muftī*, say on 2 Sha'bān 659 in the Rawaḥiyya Madrasa in Damascus, "One of the *fuqahā'* told me that a shaykh had written a book called *The Book of the End of the Quest*. I had the habit of copying down a certain number of pages during the night. One night while I was writing I looked at the lamp and found that it had very little oil. It was not enough for me to finish my work. I then got busy writing and forgot about it. I did not remember it until I had written my work and counted up the pages. When I had counted them, I remembered it and glanced at the lamp. I went out while I was looking at it."

Our Shaykh also said that the shaykh, 'Īsā al-Kurdī ash-Shāfi'ī, passed away to the mercy and pleasure of Allah in 656 AH. He was a *faqīh* at the Rawaḥiyya Madrasa in Damascus. Some days after he died, I saw him in a dream. Having known that he had died, I greeted him and then said, "May you be given life, Najmu'd-dīn!" Then I said to him, "Al-Ghazālī says in the "Book of Death" in his book, *Iḥyā' 'Ulūm ad-dīn*, that death is an immense matter. No one has ever come after death to tell about its reality, and no one recognises its reality except the one who tastes it, so tell us about its reality." He answered, "Even if it is difficult, it is only for a brief moment, and then it is over." I said, "And what is your state after it?" He answered, "There [meaning with Allah] is much good." He seems to have been indicating his excellent state by Prophet's favour, even if the mercy of Allah is deferred. At least that was my impression.

Muḥammad an-Nawawī died the same year. I recited the noble seal of the Qur'an (*Ṣūrat Yāsīn*) over him. I then saw him in a dream, may Allah have mercy on him, and I knew that he died, so I asked him, "What is your state, Shamsu'd-dīn?"

He answered, "Today we do not enter the Garden but we have other enjoyment." He meant that we would not enter the Garden until after the Last Day.

I said, "You have spoken the truth. Today no one enters the Garden except the Prophets and the martyrs. As far as other people are concerned, they have other enjoyment before the Next World comes, then they will enter the Garden after the Last Day, as the *Sharī'a* says." Then I asked him, "It has come down to us that the spirit (*rūḥ*) returns to the body before the questioning in the grave by the two angels, Munkar and Nakīr. Is its return to the body after the body has been placed in the grave or before, while the corpse is being carried on its bier?"

He answered, "It takes place after the body is placed in the grave." May Allah have mercy on him, and on our parents, and our shaykhs and whoever helps us, our companions, whoever we behave badly towards, and all the Muslims. Amen.

I heard our companion, the shaykh and scrupulous *zāhid* and gnostic, Shamsu'd-dīn, at the Samisatiyya Khanqāh in Damascus. He said that some days ago an argument had taken place between some of the shaykhs who are our companions, and he told me who they were, but I prefer not to mention that. What they were discussing were the first fragments of the copies of the Qur'ān which were considered as not having been revealed, since our companions stated that the ink itself is not the Word which is from before-endless-time. It only indicates the word. Finally, they sought the guidance of al-Juwaynī to find out what he might say about it. They met him, and then they left.

He said, "That night I had a dream. It seemed as if there were a sea, and something was in the middle of the sea which people were trying to look at. All of the scholars of the Muslims were going around it and looking at that thing, intent upon it, but they did not know what it was, nor could they perceive it. Then I saw al-Juwaynī come in between the people. He tied up his robe and walked about fifteen arm-lengths into that sea. Then he could not go any further, so he just stood there. Behind the scholars were a large group of people busy with primary knowledge, i.e. intellectual sciences like astronomy, logic and the fundamentals (*uṣūl*) of the *dīn*. There were also those occupied with argument and debate, some of those to whom is ascribed lack of the *dīn*, abandoning the prayer and wrong beliefs. I recognised them standing behind the people. Dogs were urinating on all of them. I recognised one man in particular among them whose area of expertise was dispute. He was considered to be a man totally lacking in the *dīn*. I do not want to name him. He was drunk."

This was exactly as he said. We ask Allah, the Generous, the Kind, the Master of Immensity, Power, bounty and kindness, the Merciful, the Compassionate, to make our end good, and that of our parents, shaykhs, companions, and those we love, and all the Muslims. Amen.

Abū Sa'īd as-Sam'ānī said in *The Book of Lineages* that Shaykh Abū Bakr al-Kattānī performed 12,000 *ṭawāfs* and died in 322.

As-Sam'ānī mentioned in the *Lineages* that Abū Ya'qūb Isḥāq al-Kirāmī was very good at speaking and calling people to the *dīn* — five thousand Magians became Muslim through his efforts.

Abū Bakr al-Anbarī said that Abū'l-'Abbās Aḥmad ibn Yaḥyā said that he heard 10,000 *ḥadiths* from Abū Sa'īd al-Hāshimī al-Baṣrī al-Baghdādī.

In various places I saw that the Shaykh, may Allah have have mercy on him, had written, "I heard our Shaykh, the Qāḍī and Imām of the scholars, Badru'd-dīn al-Arbīlī ash-Shāfi'ī say, 'I saw a woman, and thought that she must be someone righteous.' He meant that she had memorized all of the Qur'an in seventy days."

I heard our Shaykh al-Baṭūlisī say many times that he had counted the books which al-Ghazālī wrote and which were distributed during his lifetime. "Every day I did four pages. That is a favour of Allah which He gives to whomever He wills."

Someone who was famous for many writings was our Imam, Abū 'Abdullāh Idrīs ash-Shāfi'ī, and Abū'l-Ḥasan al-Ash'arī, may Allah be pleased with them. Al-Bayhaqī ennumerated the works of ash-Shāfi'ī and Ibn 'Asākir in his book, *Clarification of the Lies of the Fabricator.* He ascribed about 300 books to Abū'l-Ḥasan al-Ash'arī.

I heard our Shaykh, Abū Isḥāq 'Īsā al-Murādī, say on Wednesday, 7 Shawwāl 658 in the Badiraniyya Madrasa in Damascus that he heard Shaykh 'Abdu'l-'Aẓīm, may Allah have mercy on him, say, "I wrote ninety volumes in my own hand and I wrote seven hundred sections, all from the science of *ḥadīth* written by someone else." He wrote many things from his own works and the works of other people. Our Shaykh said, "I have never seen or heard anyone who strove more than he did in his occupation. He was always busy, day and night."

He said further, "I lived near him in the Madrasa in Cairo. I had a room above his for twelve years. I never woke up at any hour of the night without finding that his lamp was lit in his room and he was engaged in studying. His occupation with it was so great that even while he was eating, he had a book or two with which he was occupied."

He also mentioned some of his precision, the intensity of his investigation and its investigation and its diversity, which cannot even be properly discussed. He added, "He never left the Madrasa even for a funeral, a wedding or a wedding-feast. He never left it for anything except the *Jumu'a* prayer. All his moments were taken up in absorption with knowledge." May Allah be pleased with him, with our parents and all the Muslims.

I read that our Shaykh said, "I copies out the *Ṣaḥīḥ* of al-Bukhārī out in six volumes with one reed. Then I sharpened that reed and wrote things after al-Bukhari with it." Ibn Qutayba said in *The Adab of the Scribe,* 'I sharpened the pen, and I sharpened it well!"

Camel-driver, repeat their tale!
Hearing about them polishes the rusty heart.

I heard our Shaykh, 'Izzu'd-din Abū Ḥafs al-Arbīlī ash-Shāfi'ī say often, "Whoever does an act of obedience for Allah, the Mighty, the Majestic, is the one who remembers Allah, the Mighty, the Majestic."

*****

This is the end of the book of the *walī* of Allah, Muḥyī'd-dīn an-Nawawī, may Allah be pleased with him and with us, our parents, our shaykhs, our companions and all the Muslims. Praise be to Allah alone! May Allah bless our master Muḥammad and his family and Companions, the pure good ones, with an inseparable blessing and peace until the Day of the *Dīn*.

Glossary

abdāl: plural of *badl*, a gnostic in constant contemplation of Allah, often seen in more than one place at the same time. *Badl* means "substitute".

adab: correct behaviour, both inward and outward, good deportment. It is the deep courtesy observed in acts of worship as the person is aware that he is constantly dependent on and in the presence of Allah.

Ahl aṣ-Ṣuffa: the People of the Bench, the poor and needy among the Companions of the Prophet who lived on a verandah (*ṣuffa*) next to the house of the Prophet and the mosque in Madina.

Amir al-Mu'minīn: "the Commander of the Believers," the title of the Khalif.

Anṣār: the "Helpers", the people of Madina who welcomed and aided the Prophet and the Muhājirūn.

awliyā': the plural of *walī*.

āya(t): a verse of the Qur'ān. It literally means "sign" and also refers to the signs that one sees in Creation. (Sometimes written as *āya*, which is a more faithful representation of the Arabic.) The plural is *āyāt*.

dhikr: lit. remembrance, mention. Commonly used, it means invocation of Allah by repetition of His names or particular formulae.

Dhū'l-Qarnayn: "the two-horned", a name given to a great ruler in the past who ruled all over the world, and was a true believer. It is often thought to refer to Alexander the Great.

dīn: often written *deen*, the life-transaction, lit. the debt between two parties, in this usage between the Creator and created.

faqīh (plural *fuqahā'*)**:** a man learned in the knowledge of *fiqh* who by virtue of his knowledge can give a legal judgement.

faqīr (plural *fuqarā'*): someone who is needy or poor, used to describe someone following a spiritual tradition since the creature is poor and the Creator rich.

Fātiḥa: "the Opener," the first *sūra* of the Qur'an.

fatwā (plural *fatāwā*)**:** an authoritative statement on a point of law.

fiqh: the science of the application of the *Sharī'a*. A practitioner or expert in *fiqh* is called a *faqīh*.

fuqarā': plural of *faqīr*.

ghusl: major ablution of the whole body with water required to regain purity after menstruation, lochia and sexual intercourse.

ḥadd (plural *ḥudūd*)**:** Allah's boundary limits for the lawful and unlawful. The *ḥadd* punishments are specific fixed penalties laid down by Allah for specified crimes.

ḥadīth: reported speech of the Prophet.

ḥāfiẓ: someone who has memorised the Qur'ān.

Ḥajj: the annual pilgrimage to Makka which is one of the five pillars of Islam.

ḥalāl: lawful in the *Sharī'a*.

ḥarām: unlawful in the *Sharī'a*.

Hijra: emigration in the way of Allah. Islamic dating begins with the *Hijra* of the Prophet Muḥammad from Makka to Madina in 622 CE.

himma: spiritual aspiration, yearning to be free of illusion; highest energy impulse in a human to reconnect with reality. There are two types: *jibilla*, inborn, and acquired.

Iblīs: the personal name of the Devil. He is also called Shayṭān or the "enemy of Allah".

Ibrāhīm: the Prophet Abraham.

'Īd al-Aḍḥa: the *Ḥajj* festival which takes places on the 10th of the month of Dhū'l-Ḥijja.

'Īd al-Fiṭr: the festival at the end of the fast of Ramaḍān on the 1st of the month of Shawwāl.

iḥsān: absolute sincerity to Allah in oneself: it is to worship Allah as though you were seeing Him because He sees you.

ikhlāṣ: sincerity, pure unadulterated genuineness.

'Ishā': the night prayer.

isnād: a tradition's chain of transmission from individual to individual.

Isrā'īl: Israel, the Prophet Ya'qūb (Jacob).

Jāhilīya: the Time of Ignorance before the coming of Islam.

jihād: struggle, particularly fighting in the way of Allah to establish Islam.

Jumu'a: the day of gathering, Friday, and particularly the *Jumu'a* prayer which is performed instead of *Ẓuhr* by those who attend it.

Ka'ba: the cube-shaped building at the centre of the *Ḥaram* in Makka, originally built by the Prophet Ibrāhīm. Also known as the House of Allah.

karāmāt: marks of honour, miracles. Distinct from *mu'jizāt* – prophetic miracles, things which cannot be imitated. Both are *kharq al-'adāt*, the extraordinary breaking of normal patterns.

al-Khiḍr: or al-Khāḍir, "the green one," whose journey with Mūsā is mentioned in the Qur'ān 18:64. He may or may not be a Prophet, and appears often to people.

khirqa: a patched robe worn as a sign of poverty and devotion.

Maghrib: the sunset prayer.

Maryam: Mary, the mother of 'Īsā.

Masjid al-Ḥaram: the great mosque in Makka.

minbar: steps on which the Imam stands to deliver the *khuṭba*, or sermon, on Friday.

muftī: someone qualified to give a legal opinion or *fatwā*.

Munkar and Nakīr: the two angels who come to question a person in the grave about his or her beliefs and actions while in this world.

Mūsā: the Prophet Moses.

Mu'tazilites: someone who adheres to the school of the Mu'tazila which is rationalist in its approach to existence. Originally they held that anyone who commits a sin is neither a believer nor an unbeliever. They also held the Qur'an to be created.

nafs: the self. Usually in reference to the lower self – either the self which commands to evil, or the reproachful self.

rak'a(t): a unit of the prayer consisting of a series of standings, bowing, prostrations and sittings.

Ramaḍān: the month of fasting, the ninth month in the Muslim lunar calendar.

ribāṭ: the stronghold traditionally used by the Muslims to prepare for their *jihād* against the enemies of Islam, situated at exposed points of the frontier; later a *ṭarīqa*-based centre of religious instruction.

rūḥ: (plural *arwāḥ*) the soul, vital spirit.

rukū‘: bowing, particularly the bowing position in the prayer.

ṣadaqa: charitable giving in the Cause of Allah.

Salaf: the early generations of the Muslims.

Sharī‘a: lit. road, the legal modality of a people based on the Revelation of their Prophet. The final *Sharī‘a* is that of Islam.

ṣidq: truthfulness.

siwāk: a small stick, usually from the arak tree, whose tip is softened and used for cleaning the teeth.

Sulaymān: the Prophet Solomon.

Sunna: the customary practice of a person or group of people. It has come to refer almost exclusively to the practice of the Messenger of Allah and to the first generation of Muslims.

Tābi‘ūn: the Followers, the second generation of the early Muslims who did not meet the Prophet Muḥammad, may Allah bless him and grant him peace, but who learned the *Dīn* of Islam from his Companions.

takbīr: saying "*Allāhu Akbar*", "Allah is greater".

takbīr al-iḥrām: the *takbīr* which begins the prayer.

taqwā: awe or fear of Allah, which inspires a person to be on guard against wrong action and eager for actions which please Him.

ṭawāf: circumambulation of the Ka‘ba, done in sets of seven circuits.

tawḥīd: the doctrine of Divine Unity.

tayammum: purification for prayer with clean dust, earth, or stone, when water for *ghusl* or *wuḍū'* is either unavailable or would be detrimental to health.

uṣūl: plural of *aṣl*, the basic principles of any source, used in *fiqh*.

walī: (plural *awliyā'*) someone who is "friend" of Allah, thus possessing the quality of *wilāya*.

wilāya: friendship, in particular with Allah, referring to the *wali's* station of knowledge of the Real by direct seeing.

wuḍū': ritual washing to be pure for the prayer.

zāhid: someone whose heart has no inclination or attachment for this world.

Zakariyyā: the Prophet Zacharia, the father of Yaḥyā, John the Baptist, and guardian of Maryam.

zakāt: one of the five pillars of Islam. It is a wealth tax paid on certain forms of wealth: gold and silver, stable crops, livestock, and trading goods.

zawīya: a "corner", small mosque, or religious retreat, often where the shaykh teaches.

zuhd: making do with little of this of world and leaving what you do not need.

zuhhād: plural of *zāhid*.

Biographical Notes

'Abdullāh ibn Mas'ūd: (d. 32/652), one of the earliest Companions, renowned for his knowledge, especially about the Qur'ān and matters of *fiqh*.

'Abdullāh ibn 'Umar: *see Ibn 'Umar.*

'Abdu'r-Raḥmān ibn Mahdī: *see Ibn Mahdī.*

'Abdu'l-Wāḥid ibn Zayd: (d. ca, 177/793-4), a companion of al-Ḥasan al-Baṣrī and ad-Dārānī who stressed the importance of solitude.

Abū 'Amr (Shaykh): *see Ibn aṣ-Ṣalāḥ.*

Abū Bakr ibn Fūrak: Muḥammad ibn al-Ḥasan:, an important and very scrupulpus scholar in *fiqh*, grammar, the roots and Ash'arī *kalam*. He died of poison on his way back from Ghazna in 406/1015 and was buried in Nishapur.

Abū Dāwūd as-Sijistānī: (203/817-275/888) the compiler of the Sunan, one of the six canonical volumes of *ḥadīth*. He was one of the greatest of the scholars of *ḥadīth.*

Abū Dharr: Jundub ibn Junāda al-Ghifārī. The Prophet said about him, "The sky has not covered and the earth has not carried anyone more truthful than Abū Dharr." He also said, "May Allah have mercy on Abu Dharr! He lives alone and will die alone and will be gathered alone." He died in ar-Rabadha in 32/652.

Abū Ḥanīfa: an-Nu'mān ibn Thābit, (ca. 80/699-150/767), founder of the Ḥanafī school, one of the four Imams, a *faqīh* and *mujtahid.* He was a *ḥadīth* expert who had all the *ḥadīths* of Makka and Madina in addition to those of Kufa. He developed *ra'y* (legal opinion).

Abū Hurayra:'Abdu'r-Raḥmān ibn Ṣakhr of Daws. His pre-Muslim name was 'Abdu Shams. It is said that the Prophet gave him that *kunya* because he saw him carrying a cat in his sleeve. He became Muslim in the year of Khaybar and clung to the assembly of the Prophet and was one of the Ahl as-Suffa. He is considered to be one of the Companions with the greatest memory. He died in Madina in 58/678 at the age of 78.

Abū Isḥāq: 'Amr ibn 'Abdullāh, (d. 127/744), a great Follower and one of the scholars of *ḥadīth*. He took from a number of Companions and Followers. He fasted and prayed a lot and went on expeditions.

Abū'l-Khayr al-Aqṭa' at-Tīnātī: (d. 340/951) He came from the Maghrib and lived in a place called Tīnāt. He had many miracles and was unique in his time in his complete trust in Allah. He died in Egypt āand is buried in Qarāfa.

Abu Mas'ūd 'Uqba ibn 'Amr al-Badrī: (d. ca. 40/660), a Companion who was present at the Second Pledge of 'Aqaba. He was one of the earliest Madinan converts. He lived at Badr and died in Madina in Mu'āwiya's reign. 'Alī put him in charge of Kufa when he left for the Battle of Ṣiffīn.

Abū Muslim al-Khawlānī: 'Abdullah ibn Thuwāb, (d. ca. 62/682), one of the Followers who was devoted to worship. He was a *faqīh* and ascetic. In the Yemen, the false Prophet al-Aswad threw him into a fire and he was saved from it. He emigrated while Abū Bakr was khalif and settled in Syria. He is called "the sage of this Community".

Abū Sa'īd al-Baghdādī al-Kharrāz: (d. ca. 286/899) Aḥmad ibn 'Isā of Baghdad, a Sufi and a cobbler by trade, author of *Kitab aṣ-Ṣidq* and other books.

Abū Sa'īd al-Khudrī: Sa'īd ibn Mālik ibn Sinān, (d. ca. 74/693) an important Companion, one of the Anṣār of Khazraj, who took part in twelve battles with the Prophet. He died in Madina and was buried in al-Baqi'.

Abū Sulaymān ad-Dārānī: 'Abdu'r-Raḥmān, (d. 205/820-1), renowned among the Sufis for his piety and self-mortification. He left a number of sayings, like 'The sign of destruction is the drying-up of tears."

Abū Tha'laba: (d. 75/685), a Companion who moved Syria.

Abū 'Uthmān al-Maghribī: Sa'īd ibn Sallām al-Maghribī. (d. 373/983-4), a well-known Sufi born in Qayrawān who travelled to the east.

Abū 'Uthmān an-Nahdī: 'Abdu'r-Raḥmān ibn Mull, (d. ca. 100/719), a Follower, who was a reliable transmitter of *ḥadīth*.

Abū Yaḥyā Zakariyyā ibn Yaḥyā as-Sājī: (307/919) a *ḥadīth* scholar in Baṣra who wrote a books on defects in *ḥadīths*. He was almost 90 when he died.

Abū Yūsuf: Ya'qūb ibn Ibrāhīm ibn Habib al-Baghdādī, (113/731 - 182/798). Born in Kufa, he became one of the main students of Abū Ḥanīfa and the first to propagate his school. He was a *ḥadīth* master and brilliant jurist with an extensive knowledge of *tafsīr*. He acted as qāḍī in Baghdad for the khalifs, al-Mahdī, al-Hādī and Hārūn ar-Rashīd.

Aḥmad ibn Abī'l-Ḥawārī: Abū'l-Ḥasan, (d. c. 230/844-5), an early Syrian or perhaps Kufan Sufi, a disciple of ad-Dārānī and companion of Ibn 'Uyayna. He is said to have thrown away his books and lived the life of a wandering ascetic.

Aḥmad ibn Ḥanbal: (164/780-241/856), Imām of the Ahl as-Sunna, the founder of the Ḥanbalī school and compiler of a *Musnad* which contains 30,000 *ḥadīths*.

'Ā'isha: (d. 58/678) the daughter of Abū Bakr aṣ-Ṣiddiq and favourite wife of the Prophet.

'Alī ibn Naṣr: Abū'l-Ḥasan al-Jahdamī, (d. 250/864), a *ḥadīth* scholar of Baṣra.

'Alqama ibn Waqqāṣ: (d. after 80/699), a Follower who is a reliable transmitter of *ḥadīth*.

al-A'mash : Abū Muḥammad Sulaymān ibn Mihrān al-A'mash, (61/680-147/764), a famous Follower whose family came from Rayy. He was a prominent scholar in *tafsīr, ḥadīth* and shares of inheritance. He grew up in Kufa and died there.

'Ammār ibn Yasār al-Kinānī: Abū'l-Yaqaẓān, (d. 37/657), a famous Companion. He was one of the first to become Muslim and openly state it. He emigrated to Madina and was present at the battles of Badr, Uhud, the Ditch and the Pledge of Riḍwān. The Prophet called him "*aṭ-ṭayyib al-muṭayyib* (the pleasant and good)". He was the first to build a mosque in Islam. He was present at the Battles of the Camel and Ṣiffīn with 'Alī, being killed in Ṣiffīn at the age of 93.

'Amr ibn Shuraḥbīl al-Hamdānī: Abū Maysara, (d. ca. 59/678), one of the Followers in Kūfa who transmitted *ḥadīths*.

Anas ibn Mālik: (d. ca. 93/711) the famous Companion. He served the Prophet when he was eight or ten years old and stayed with him for twenty years. 2206 *ḥadīths* are reported from him. He died when he was 100 years old and was buried near Baṣra.

al-Ash'arī: Abū'l-Ḥasan 'Alī ibn Ismā'īl (260/873-4 -324 /936). He was for a time a Mu'tazilite, a follower of al-Jubbā'i, but later left them. He became an unrivalled great scholar, the Imām of the People of the Sunna in *kalām*. He wrote about 300 books. In his *Maqālāt al-Islāmiyīn*, the first book of its kind, he goes into detail about the different sects. He and al-Māturīdī are the founders of Sunnī *kalām*.

al-Aswad: a title of 'Ayhala ibn Ka'b, also known as Dhū'l-Khimâr (the Veiled), a false Prophet in southwest Arabia at the end of the Prophet's life. He was assassinated in a power struggle.

'Aṭā' ibn Yasār: Abū Muḥammad al-Madanī, (d. 94/715 or 93/721) one of the great Followers.

al-Bayhaqī: Aḥmad ibn al-Ḥusayn, Abū Bakr, (d. 458/1066), a famous scholar who produced nearly 1,000 volumes. He was one of the great Imāms in *ḥadīth* and Shāfi'ī *fiqh*. He wrote some important books, such *as-Sunan al-Kubrā, as-Sunan as-Sughrā, al-Mabsūṭ*, and *al-Asmā' wa'ṣ-Ṣifāt*.

Bishr ibn al-Ḥārith: Abū Naṣr ibn al-Ḥārith al-Ḥāfī, (150/767-227/841), he renounced a life of dissipation and studied *ḥadīth* in Baghdad and then became a mendicant. He was much admired by Aḥmad ibn Ḥanbal.

al-Bisṭāmī: Abū Yazid Ṭayfūr ibn 'Isā, known as Bayazīd al-Bistāmī. (188/804.-260/874) a famous Sufi in the east. He made a detailed study of the *Sharī'a* and practiced self-denial (*zuhd*). He is famous for his ecstatic expressions. He died at the age of 71.

al-Bukhārī: Abū 'Abdullāh Muḥammad ibn Ismā'īl, (194/810-256/870), the famous *ḥadīth* scholar, who produced the *Ṣaḥīḥ* Collection. He said that he produced the *Ṣaḥīḥ* from the cream of 6,000 *ḥadīths*, and did not write down any *ḥadīth* in it until he had first prayed two *rak'ats*.

ad-Daqqāq: Abū 'Alī, (d. 405/1014), the Imām of the Sufis of his time and the shaykh of Abū'l-Qāsim al-Qushayrī. Originally from Nishapur, he studied there, after which he travelled to Marw, where he studied Shāfi'ī *fiqh*.

ad-Dāraquṭnī : 'Alī ibn 'Umar, (306/918-385/995) from Dār al-Quṭn, a part of Baghdad. He was an unrivalled scholar in his era. He had knowledge of traditions and weaknesses and the names of the men and their states in integrity, truthfulness and knowledge of the schools of the *fuqahā'*. He had several books, including a *ḥadīth* collection, *as-Sunan*, and *al-Istidrāk* which is about the weakness of some *ḥadīths* in al-Bukhārī.

ad-Dārimī: Abū Muḥammad 'Abdullāh ibn 'Abdu'r-Raḥmān at-Tamīmī, (181/797-8 -255/869) a scholar famous for his integrity and scrupulousness. His students included Muslim, Abū Dāwūd, at-Tirmidhī and an-Nasā'ī. He was appointed qāḍī of Samarqand, judged one case and then resigned. He produced a *Sunan*.

Dhū'n-Nūn al-Miṣrī: Abū'l-Fayḍ Thawbān ibn Ibrāhīm, (ca. 180/796-245/860), the ascetic and Sufi. Of Nubian origin, he studied under several teachers and travelled extensively through Arabia and Syria. In 214/829 al-Mutawakkil accused him of heresy but having listened to him, released him. He is said to be the first to have given a systematic explanation of the states (*aḥwāl*) and stations (*maqāmāt*) on the spiritual path.

ad-Duqqī: Abū Bakr Muḥammad ad-Dīnawarī, (d. 363/974), Sufi of Syria who died when over 100 years old.

Fuḍayl ibn 'Iyāḍ: Abū 'Alī aṭ-Ṭālaqānī, (d.187/803) He was a highwayman at the beginning of his life. Then he repented and went to Makka and then to Kufa where he resided for many years. He had a reputation as an authority in *ḥadīth* which he studied under Sufyān ath-Thawrī and Abū Ḥanīfa. He likened this world to a madhouse.

al-Ghazalī: (also written al-Ghazzālī) Muḥammad ibn Muḥammad, Abū Ḥamid aṭ-Ṭūsī, (450/1058 -505/1111), the Shāfi'ī Imām and Sufi. He studied *fiqh* with al-Juwaynī. He taught at the Niẓāmiyya Madrasa before he became a Sufi, pointing out that all religious certainty was a result of spiritual experience. He is nicknamed "Shāfi'ī the Second". He was the author of many books, especially *Iḥyā' 'Ulūm ad-Dīn.*

Ḥabīb ibn 'Abī Thābit: (d. 119/737) a Follower who was a *muftī* in Kufa and is considered reliable.

al-Hajjāj ibn Yūsuf: Abū Muḥammad, (41/661-95/714), a clever and bloodthirsty general and orator. He ruled Iraq with an iron fist for 'Abdu'l-Mālik ibn Marwān.

Ḥammād ibn Salama: Abū Salama al-Baṣrī, (d. 167/783), the *muftī* of Baṣra and a reliable narrator of *ḥadīth*, excellent in Arabic and opposition to innovation.

al-Ḥārith al-Muḥāsibī: (165/781-243/857) He was called al-Muḥāsibī because he frequently called himself to account (*muḥāsaba*) and because of his asceticism. He was an excellent scholar, held in high esteem among the people of his time in both outward and inward knowledge, and wrote many books.

al-Ḥasan ibn 'Alī: (3/625 - 50/670) the son of 'Alī and Fāṭima, the eldest grandson of the Prophet.

Hilāl ibn al-'Alā': Abū 'Amra, (d. 280/ 893), *ḥadīth* scholar of north-eastern Syria.

Hisham ibn 'Abdi'l-Malik: (105/724-125/743), Umayyad khalif.

Ḥudhayfa al-Mar'ashī: (d. 207/ 822), a Sufi and companion of Ibrāhīm ibn Adham.

al-Ḥusayn b. 'Alī: the second son of 'Alī and Fatima, killed at Karbalā in 61/680.

Ibn 'Abbās: 'Abdullāh ibn 'Abbās, (d. 68/687-8), a cousin and close Companion of the Prophet. He is known as the greatest scholar of the first generation of the Muslims. He narrated many *ḥadīths* and is the founder of the science of *tafsīr.*

Ibn Abī'd-Dunyā: (d. 281/894) a Sufi in Baghdad He wrote a book entitled *Dhamm ad-Dunyā* ("Censuring this world").

Ibn Mahdī: 'Abdu'r-Raḥmān al-Baṣrī, known as al-Lu'lu'ī, (d.198/813), a reliable *ḥadīth* scholar. Ibn al-Madinī said, "Ibn Mahdī is the person with the greatest knowledge of *hadith.*" Az-Zuhrī said, "I never saw a book in his hand," i.e. he knew his *hadith* by heart.

Ibn aṣ-Ṣalāḥ: Abū 'Amr 'Uthmān ibn 'Abdu'r-Raḥmān ash-Shāhrazūrī, known as Ibn aṣ-Ṣalāḥ. (577/1181-643/1245), an important Shāfi'ī scholar. He wrote a number of books on various topics, including *fiqh*. He has a famous collection of *fatwās* called *Fatāwā Ibn aṣ-Ṣalāḥ.*

Ibn Mājah: Abū 'Abdullāh Muḥammad ibn Yazid al-Qazwīnī, (209/824-273/886), a *ḥadīth* master who compiled the *Sunan*, one of the six major collections of *ḥadīth*.

Ibn Qutayba: (d. 276/889), Iraqi scholar.

Ibn as-Sunnī: Abū Bakr ibn Muḥammad ad-Dīnawarī, (d. 364/974), the *mawlā* of Ja'far ibn Abī Ṭālib. He wrote, "The Actions of the Day and Night" and transmitted the *Sunan* of an-Nasā'ī.

Ibn 'Umar: 'Abdullāh, (d. 73/693), a Companion of the Prophet, son of 'Umar ibn al-Khaṭṭāb. He enjoyed universal respect because of his character and knowledge.

Ibrāhīm ibn Dā'ud ar-Raqqī: Abū Isḥāq, (d. 326/938), a Sufi shaykh of Syria and one of the people of al-Junayd.

Ibrāhīm ibn Adham: Abū Isḥāq at-Tamīmī al-Balkhī, (d. 161/778), an early Sufi *zāhid* and *walī*. Born into a wealthy family of Balkh, he gave it all up to seek knowledge through travel, taking on all sorts of menial jobs and fighting in the *jihād* against the Byzantines. He attended the gatherings of Sufyān ath-Thawrī.

'Irbād ibn Sārīya as-Sulamī: (d. 75/695), a famous Companion who became Muslim early on and was one of the *Ahl aṣ-Suffa*. He is one of those about whom it was revealed, *"... neither against those who, when they came to you, for you to mount them, and you said, 'I do not find anything on which to mount you,' turned away with their eyes overflowing with tears."* (9:92)

al-Isfarāyinī, Abū Isḥāq: Ibrāhīm ibn Muḥammad, (d. 418/1027), scholar in *fiqh* and *uṣūl*. He built a great madrasa in Nisapur where he taught. He was famous and reliable in the transmission of *ḥadīth*.

Jābir ibn 'Abdullāh: al-Khazrajī, (d. c. 78/697), a Companion. He related 1500 *ḥadīths* and taught in the Prophet's Mosque.

Ja'far ibn Muḥammad al-Khuldī: (d. 348/959/60), a major Sufi of Baghdad, companion of Ruwaym, al-Junayd and an-Nūrī who spent most of his life travelling. His aphorisms are much quoted and his book, *Ḥikāyāt al-Awliyā'*, was famous in its time.

Jarīr ibn 'Abdullāh al-Bajalī al-Anṣārī: (d. 51/671-2),a Companion who came to the Prophet in 10/632. He had great influence in the victory of Qādisiyya. Then he settled in Kufa.

al-Junayd: Abū'l-Qāsim ibn Muḥammad, (d. 297/910), the great shaykh of Sufism. His *fiqh* was taken from Abū Thawr and Sufyān ath-Thawrī. He took his *ṭarīqa* from as-Sarī as-Saqaṭī, his uncle, and al-Muḥasibī. He was one of the Shāfi'ī *fuqahā'* and is buried in Baghdad.

al-Juwaynī: Abū'l-Ma'ālī 'Abdu'l-Mālik ibn 'Abdullāh, Imām of the Two Ḥarams, and the the shaykh of al-Ghazālī, (d. 478/1085) He was the outstanding Ash'arite *mutakallim* of his time and introduced al-Ghazālī to *kalām*. His Ash'arite treatise is entitled *al-Irshād.*

al-Kattānī: Shaykh Abū Bakr Muḥammad ibn 'Alī, (d. 322/933-4), a Baghdad Sufi of the circle of al-Junayd and al-Kharrāz. He spent much of his life in Makka, where he died.

al-Khalīl ibn Aḥmad: (d. 170/786), famous grammarian and teacher of Sibuwayh, who compiled the first Arabic dictionary and is credited with the formulation of the rules of Arabic prosody. He introduced the traditional vowel signs into Arabic.

al-Khaṭṭāb: Abū Sulaymān Ḥamd, (d. 308/920), a leader in all branches of knowledge, especially *ḥadīth*, *fiqh* and literature. He was a Shāfi'ī who wrote several books.

Khubayb ibn 'Adi al-Ansari: (d. 4/625) a Companion sent on the ar-Rajī' expedition, he was captured and sold in Makka to the sons of al-Ḥārith ibn 'Āmir, whom he had killed at Badr. They took him to Tan'īm where he prayed two *rak'ats* and then they killed him.

al-Madā'inī: 'Abū'l-Ḥasan 'Alī ibn Muḥammad, (ca. 132/749-50 - 224 or 225/839/840), a famous early historian. He wrote a history on the khalifs and a book on campaigns, both of which are lost.

Makḥūl: ibn Abi Muslim, Abū 'Abdullāh, (d. 112/730), the most renowned scholar of Syria in his time, he was a freed slave who studied and travelled in search of knowledge and was famous for *fatwā.*

Mālik ibn Anas: (d. 179/795), the famous Imām of Madina in *fiqh* and *ḥadīth*. One of the four Imams, founder of the Mālikī school and author of the *Muwattā'*.

al-Ma'mūn: Abū'l-'Abbās 'Abdullāh (170/786 - 218/833), the seventh 'Abbasid caliph (198-218/813-833).

Ma'rūf al-Karkhī: al-Karkhī: Abū Maḥfūẓ ibn Fīrūz, (d. 200/815-6) a famous Sufi of the Baghdad school. He had a great influence on as-Sarī as-Saqaṭī, whose shaykh he was, and taught *ḥadīth* to Ibn Ḥanbal.

Mu'āwiya ibn Abī Sufyān: (d. 60/680), a Companion and founder of the Umayyad dynasty. He became khalif in 40/661.

al-Muḥāmilī: Qāḍī Abū 'Abdullāh al-Ḥusayn ibn Ismā'īl, (d. 235/850-330 /942) Shaykh of Baghdad and *ḥadīth* scholar. He was appoined qāḍī of Kūfa in 260/874. He had a circle of *fiqh* in Kufa.

Muḥammad ibn Ibrāhīm at-Taymī: al-Madinī, Abū 'Abdullāh, (d. 120/738) a Follower and trustworthy and esteemed imam.

Muḥammad ibn Sulaymān al-Hāshimī: ibn 'Alī ibn 'Abdullāh ibn 'Abbās, (d. 173/789-90), the governor of Baṣra for a time.

Mujāhid: Abū Muḥammad ibn Jabr, (21/642 -104/722), one of the great Followers renowned for his knowledge of *tafsīr* which he learned from Ibn 'Abbās with whom he went over the Qur'an three times, stopping at every verse to ask about it. The authors of the *Sunan* and others transmit from him. *Ḥadīth* scholars consider him reliable.

Muqātil ibn Ṣāliḥ al-Khurāsānī: (d. 150/767) Although he is renowned for his knowledge of *tafsīr*, and his *tafsīr* appears to be the earliest in existence, he is often viewed unfavourably, but the reason is not entirely clear. He was a Zaydī and Murji'ite.

Muslim: Abū'l-Ḥusayn Muslim ibn al-Ḥajjāj al-Qushayrī an-Nīsābūrī, (204/820- 261/875, a Shāfi'ī scholar and *ḥadīth* master. He composed his *Ṣaḥīḥ* Collection from 3,000 *ḥadīths*, and it is said to be the soundest book of *ḥadīth*.

al-Muzanī: Abū Ibrāhīm ibn Ismā'īl, (175/791-264/878), a Shāfi'ī *mujtahid*, he wrote *al-Mukhtaṣar* about Shāfi'ī *fiqh*. Ash-Shāfi'ī said about him, "If he had debated with Shayṭān, he would have defeated him."

an-Nasā'ī: Abū 'Abdu'r-Raḥmān Aḥmad ibn 'Alī ibn Shu'ayb, (215/830-303/915),a Shāfi'ī who wrote on the rites of *ḥajj* according to the Shāfi'ites, but is best known for his knowledge in the science of *ḥadīth* and compiled one of the six sound Collections of *ḥadīth*: the *Sunan*. His *Sunan* is the one with the fewest weak *ḥadīths* after the two mosr famous *Ṣaḥīḥ* collections.

an-Nu'mān ibn Bashīr: son of an Anṣārī Companion. Mu'āwiya appointed him governor over Ḥims and Kufa. After Mu'āwiya's death, offered his allegiance to az-Zubayr and was killed in 64/683.

Qāsim al-Jū'ī : ibn 'Uthmān ad-Dimishqī, an ascetic and worker of miracles. His name "Ju'i" derives from hunger (*ju'*).

al-Qushayrī: Abū'l-Qāsim 'Abdu'l-Karīm ibn Hawāzin, (376/986 - 465/1074), a well known scholar who wrote several books, the most famous of which is the *Risāla al-Qushayrīya* about Sufism and the biographies of the Sufis, and the *Laṭā'if al-Ishārāt* on *tafsīr*. In *kalām* he was the student of the Ash'arite, Abū Bakr ibn Fūrak, and in Sufism the follower of as-Sulamī and Abū 'Alī ad-Daqqāq.

ar-Rabī' ibn Sulaymān al-Murādī: Abū Muḥammad, (d. 270/884) a long-standing student and the main transmitter of ash-Shāfi'ī's books. He was known as "the *mu'adhdhin*" because he gave the *adhān* in the Fusṭāṭ mosque until his death.

Ribī' ibn Khirāsh: al-Ghaṭafānī, (d. 101/ 720) a scholar of action in Kufa who transmitted *ḥadīths*. He was present at al-Jābiya when 'Umar ibn al-Khaṭṭāb visited Syria to accept the surrender of Jerusalem.

ar-Rūdhbārī: Abu 'Abdullāh Ahmad ibn 'Aṭā', (d. 370/980), a Sufi in Syria.

Sa'd ibn Ibrāhīm: (d. 127/745) He was qāḍī of Madīna and died there at the age of 72.

Sahl ibn 'Abdullāh at-Tustarī: (200/815-282/896), a Sufi shaykh and ascetic, he also wrote a short *tafsīr*. He had famous miracles (*karāmāt*) and kept the company of Dhū'n-Nūn al-Miṣrī.

Sahl ibn Sa'īd: (d. 91/710) one of the famous Companions. It is said that his name was Ḥuzn (sadness) and the Prophet changed it. Az-Zuhri said the Prophet, may Allah bless him and grant him peace, died when Sahl was 15. He was the last of the Companions to die in Madina.

Sa'īd ibn Jubayr: al-Asadī, (d. 95 /714), one of the Followers and one of the scholars and transmitters of *ḥadīth* in Kufa. He related from Ibn 'Abbās, Ibn 'Umar and others and the authors of the *Sunan* related from him. He was known for his scrupulousness.

Salmān al-Fārisī: Abū 'Abdullah, the client of the Prophet and Companion. He was from Iṣfahān and did not leave the Prophet after he was set free. He called himself "Salmān al-Islām". He that he lived to a great age and died in al-Mada'in and was buried there in 35/656 or 36/657. The Messenger of Allah said of him, "The Garden yearns for him."

as-Sam'ānī: Abū Sa'd, (505-562/1113-1167). He wrote a 20 volume collection of biographies of traditionists of Marw.

as-Sari as-Saqaṭī : Abū'l-Ḥasan ibn Mughallis, (d. 253/867), said to be a pupil of Ma'rūf al-Karkhī, one of the Baghdad circle of Sufis. He was the maternal uncle and teacher of al-Junayd and one of the first to present Sufism in an organised form.

as-Sarrāj: Abū Naṣr 'Abdullāh ibn 'Alī, (d. 378/988), author of *Kitāb al-Luma'*, a classic Sufi text. He died in He studied with al-Khuldī and ad-Duqqī.

Shaddād ibn Aws: a Companion who settled in Jerusalem and died in Syria in 58/678.

ash-Shāfi'ī: Muḥammad ibn Idrīs, (150/767-204/820), the famous scholar and founder of one of the four major schools of *fiqh*. He wrote *al-Umm* and *ar-Risāla*. He was the first to formulate various legal principles, including that of abrogating and abrogated verses.

Shu'ba ibn al-Ḥajjāj: Abū Bisṭām al-'Ataki, (82/701- 160/776), a reliable narrator. He was the first to search in Iraq for knowledge of the reliability of transmitters. Ash-Shāfi'ī said, "If not for Shu'ba, *ḥadīth* would have been unknown in Iraq."

Sufyān ath-Thawrī: (d.161/778), a scholar famous for asceticism and *ḥadīth*. The Six Imāms transmitted from him. He studied under 600 shaykhs and founded a school of *fiqh*.

Sufyān ibn 'Uyayna: (d. 198/813), one of the scholars and Imams from whom the compilers of the six *Ṣaḥīḥ* collections all transmitted.

as-Sulamī: Abū 'Abdu'r-Rahman Muḥammad ibn al-Ḥusayn, (325/936 - 412/1021), a shaykh of the Sufis and author of a book on their history, ranks and *tafsīr*. He wrote the *Ṭabaqāt aṣ-Ṣūfiyya*.

Sulaymān ibn Ḥarb: al-Azdī al-Baṣrī, Qāḍī of Makka, (d. 224/839) He had knowledge of *fiqh* and the men of *ḥadīth* and was reliable. His discourses in Baghdad were attended by 40,000 people.

at-Ṭabarānī: Sulaymān ibn Aḥmad, Abu'l-Qāsim, (260/873-360/971), a *ḥadīth* master and Qur'ānic commentator who met about a thousand shaykhs of transmission, travelling for thirty-three years. He produced three *ḥadīth* collections.

Ṭalḥa ibn Muṣarrif: Abū 'Abdullāh: (d. 112/730), a scholar and Qur'an reciter in Kufa. When he saw a lot of people gathering to him, he went to al-A'mash and read to him, and so the people left Ṭalḥa for al-A'mash.

Tamīm ad-Dārī: (n.d) a Companion who moved to Syria after 'Uthman's murder. He was from the People of the Book who knew their books and had read in them that the Messenger of Allah, may Allah bless him and grant him peace, would be sent.

Thābit ibn Aslam al-Bunānī: Abū Muḥammad al-Baṣrī, (d. 127/745), the Six Collections transmit from the leader of the men of knowledge and worship in his time.

at-Tirmidhī: 'Īsā ibn Muḥammad, (209/824 - 279/892), one of the great scholars. He was proficient in *fiqh* and had many books on the science of hadith. His book *aṣ-Ṣaḥīḥ* is one of the Six.

Ubayy ibn Ka'b: al-Anṣāri, (d. ca. 32/652), a Companion and Master of the Qur'ān reciters. He was the first to write for the Prophet.

'Umar ibn al-Khaṭṭāb: the Amīr al-Mu'minīn, (d. 23/644), one of the strongest defenders of Islam and greatest Companions. He became khalif after Abu Bakr and was murdered ten and a half years later.

'Utba ibn Farqad: Abū 'Abdullāh, (n.d), a Companion. He built a house and mosque in Mosul where he was governor. He settled in Kufa.

al-Wāḥidī: Abū'l-Ḥasan 'Ali ibn Aḥmad, (d. 468/1076), has a classical *tafsir* on which as-Suyūṭī drew extensively.

Yaḥyā ibn Mu'ādh ar-Rāzī: (d. 258/871-/2), a Sufi who taught in Central Asia, one of the first to teach Sufism in mosques. He left a number of books and sayings. He emphasised *raja'* (hope).

Yaḥyā ibn Sa'īd al-Anṣārī: Abū Sa'id al-Anṣārī an-Najjārī, (d. 143/760) originally of Makka, a *qāḍī* in Madina and then in Iraq. A major figure in the early science of *ḥadīth.*

Yazīd ibn Hārūn: Abū Khālid as-Sulamī, (128/746-206/821) a reliable transmitter of *ḥadīths*. He taught in Baghdad and his circle was attended by 70,000 people.

Yūsuf ibn al-Ḥusayn: ar-Rāzī, (d. 304/916), an early Sufi in Rayy who was a disciple of Dhū'n-Nūn al-Miṣrī.

az-Zajjāj: Abū Isḥāq Ibrāhīm ibn Muḥammad, (306/918), Shaykh of Arabic and author of a fampus *tafsīr*.

az-Zaqqāq: Abū Bakr Aḥmad ibn Naṣr, famous early Sufi in Egypt, a contemporary of al-Junayd.

www.ingramcontent.com/pod-product-compliance
Lightning Source LLC
Chambersburg PA
CBHW051815040426
42446CB00007B/688
* 9 7 8 1 9 0 8 8 9 2 6 2 1 *